THE VILLAGE CULTURE IN TRANSITION

# THE VILLAGE CULTURE IN TRANSITION

A Study of East Pakistan Rural Society

*by S. M. Hafeez Zaidi*

*East-West Center Press*    *Honolulu*

Published in 1970 by East-West Center Press, University of Hawaii
All rights reserved
International Standard Book Number: 0-8248-0086-9
Library of Congress Catalog Card Number: 71-88247
Printed and bound in Hong Kong
First Edition

# PREFACE

THE MOTIVATION for writing this book came from the realization that there is no systematic information available about the village society of East Pakistan. The awareness of this deficiency grew sharper when, as a member of the faculty of the Pakistan Academy for Rural Development, Comilla, I was required to teach the principles of social behavior to the middle-range officers of the government. I felt extremely inadequate in talking about theoretical principles only remotely relevant in their training. In many cases these officers knew more about the villagers than many of the faculty members of the Academy. Their knowledge, however, was mostly general and impressionistic, although based on more direct contact with the villagers than any of us had.

With this initial interest in collecting systematic data for my own professional efficiency, the motivation to know more about the problems of village life grew with greater involvement in the action programs of rural development, which were the primary focus of the Academy. As a social scientist, my interest in the actual development activities was, of necessity, academic and limited. This restriction, I feel, made it possible for me to make more objective observations while participating directly in the action programs.

This book, therefore, is the result of my learning experience at the Academy. Indeed, in attempting to provide information to others, I have myself benefited greatly in understanding the villagers' perception of things. I may as well confess that my perspective of the rural problems has changed considerably since I started working on this book.

I do not wish to describe the book here, except to say that it is a general survey of the social-psychological aspects of village life in East Pakistan. It does not follow any specific theoretical position, although the results may be evaluated profitably within the "stress-disorganization-readjustment-steady-state" sequence (Wallace, 1961). As a general assumption, we may state that sociocultural changes in tradition-oriented societies constitute situations of stress leading to disequilibrium in the culture and its social institutions (Zaidi, 1966). A culture under stress then makes adjustments; but in the process of attaining a steady state, the values, beliefs, and attitudes of the people may suffer much modification and even distortion. It is assumed that East Pakistan village culture is at present undergoing the stress of various social changes, and is in the process of transition from disorganization to reorganization and steady state. The reactions of the villagers to this transition may, therefore, be interpreted as the reactions of a group under stress. A more detailed discussion of this general assumption is presented in the last chapter.

Within the meager systematic information available on Pakistan villages in general is some about the demographic and economic aspects of the villages. However, it barely touches upon the sociologic aspects of life in the village. The two books dealing with social behavior patterns of Pakistan villagers—Stanley Maron's *Pakistan Society* and Z. Eglar's *Punjabi Village in Pakistan*—have been written by foreign scholars. The former is a collection of papers by authors many of whom have only slight acquaintance with our village life. Moreover, the book attempts to cover a wide area and, therefore, suffers from unreliable generalizations with scanty data. The latter, though a systematic study, confines itself only to the Punjab village in West Pakistan, and, therefore, gives no insight into village life in East Pakistan. A third mimeographed monograph by J. J. Honigmann (1958) is concerned with ethnographic accounts of three villages, also in West Pakistan. Nazmul Karim's

*Changing Society in India and Pakistan* (1961) deals with East Pakistan village life in a historical perspective.

Anthropological observations by foreign scholars have a certain advantage of objectivity, but it is more than offset by the absence of the valuable experience of "living with the observed behavior." A foreign observer, even with the closest association with the subjects of his study, could not enter the "spirit of the situation" or the "inner world of meaning," and would always be left with the peripheral observations which, possibly scientific in the most rigorous sense, would represent only the mere outlines of the society.

The primary purpose of the present book, therefore, is to furnish authentic and carefully observed materials to the student of Pakistan village society. Since there is very little material of a sociopsychological nature, this book hopefully may help to fill the gap in our knowledge of the rural society of East Pakistan.

Secondly, since the village socioeconomic scene is changing fast under the impact of urbanization and industrialization, it is important to record the sociocultural situation as it exists today. We have been placed, by fate or by circumstance, in the midst of a sociocultural revolution, whereby the old values and beliefs are being transformed gradually. East Pakistan rural society is an amalgam of Hindu-Muslim traditions and customs, and, therefore, represents a unique phenomenon from a sociologic point of view. As an example of this complex integration of Hindu-Muslim cultures, one may take the caste system. Theoretically, there is no cast among Muslims. Islam terminated the basis of discrimination between man and man because of birth, color, or class. Hinduism, on the other hand, is based on caste distinctions owing to birth. But curiously, even among Muslims in many parts of India and Pakistan, social stratification is generally patterned after the Hindu caste system (Barth, 1962). This situation does not prevail in the villages of East Pakistan, although most villages of West Pakistan, especially in the Punjab, have quite rigid class distinctions (Inayatullah, 1958). A study of such a social group may have, therefore, certain theoretical implications for sociologists. This is another purpose the book may serve. It may also serve as a useful guide and help to avoid many methodological pitfalls in the design and conduct of social research in a semiliterate, tradition-oriented rural society. The picture of village life presented here is as broad-based as it was possible to paint with the available data.

The Appendix, which lists the household articles of an average village family, and the Glossary are expected to give a better understanding of village life to foreign readers. The arrangement of the nine chapters has followed the logical sequence of beginning with the family as the nucleus of village life, going on to the village in terms of its social structure and value system, and then projecting the villagers' image of the outside world and the sources of building this image.

The help and contributions of persons and institutions at various stages in preparation of the book are gratefully acknowledged in the following paragraphs.

Akhtar Hameed Khan, director of the Pakistan Academy for Rural Development: it was through his persistent but sympathetic encouragement that the foundation for the book was laid.

Edgar A. Schuler, professor of sociology, Michigan State University, and former senior advisor to the Pakistan Academy for Rural Development: it is almost impossible to document adequately Mr. Schuler's contribution to this book. Initially, it was our plan to write the book jointly, which was not possible because both of us left the Academy for different places. Mr. Schuler was very closely associated with the building up of the research instruments used in both the research and the field work. Thus, from the stage of planning up to working in the field, his contribution has been equal to, if not greater than, mine. This debt is gratefully acknowledged.

Among the institutions to be acknowledged, the Pakistan Academy at Comilla is first. The field work for the book was financed with funds from the Academy. Second in time, but no less important, is the Institute of Advance Projects, East-

West Center. Without an invitation from the I.A.P. to be a senior specialist in residence at Honolulu, this book may not have seen the light of day. It would certainly have taken much more time to complete the writing. I am extremely grateful to the authorities of the Institute of Advanced Projects for the facilities provided to me in connection with the writing of this book.

S. M. Hafeez Zaidi

*Honolulu, Hawaii*
*June 15, 1967*

# CONTENTS

# Tables

THE VILLAGE CULTURE IN TRANSITION

# CHAPTER I

# INTRODUCTION

MUSLIM political power was established in Bengal towards the beginning of the thirteenth century, although the earliest Muslim contacts with this part of the subcontinent may be dated back to the eighth century, A.D., when Arab sailors and traders started frequenting the coast of Bengal in the course of their trading activities. The spread of Islam, in the true sense, however, began with the Turkish conquest of the area. Turkish inroads towards the east of the subcontinent had started earlier, but it was in the beginning of the thirteenth century that Bengal came under them.

Mohammad Bakhtiyar Khilji drove the Brahmins and nobles of the court of King Lakhshaman Sen from Nadia (now a district in West Bengal), and they fled in different directions. After Bakhtiyar Khilji died, his successors began to extend their frontiers at the cost of neighboring Hindu principalities, but it took the Muslims more than two hundred years to bring the whole of Bengal under their control.

The Turkish conquest of Bengal served as the nucleus for a large-scale Muslim immigration, which, along with the Muslim domination over Bengal and Assam, had far-reaching effects on the socioreligious life of the people. The first and the foremost of these effects was the spread of Islam all over the area and beyond in the neighboring province of Arakan, Burma.

The three most important forces to help in the spread of Islam to the common people were the rulers, the Muslim scholars and jurists, and the *sufis* (Muslim mystics). The rulers not only expanded their political authority but also encouraged the scholars and *sufis* in scholarly pursuits and religious propagation. The rulers built mosques and established *madrasahs* and *khankahs*. The mosques provided facilities for saying prayers, the *madrasahs* educated the people in religious sciences, and the *khankahs* provided shelter and encouraged saints and holy men in their religious pursuits. The rulers also granted lands, stipends, and other pecuniary help to the scholars and *sufis*. As a result, these scholars and devotees were made free to pursue their scholarly and religious activities. The contribution of *sufis* to the spread of Islam was even greater. The *sufis* were not indifferent to the political happenings, and in their own way, influenced the rulers in molding the state policies on Islamic lines. Some *sufis* even helped in the expansion of the Muslim rule by waging *jihad* (holy war) against the infidels. The most important contribution of the *sufis*, however was that they educated the people. They preached Islam, helped the poor and the destitute, attracted people by their simplicity and devotion, and converted many to Islam.

Through the efforts of the rulers, the scholars, and the *sufis*, Muslim society in Bengal developed to such an extent that very soon it occupied a dominant position in the sociocultural life of the people. Islam became and remained the religion of the people during all these centuries.

Muslim society in Bengal developed orthodox principles of Islam, and at the same time, gave way to popular forces. The society looked for its strength to the religious institutions of the mosque, the *madrasah,* and the *khankah*. These institutions served as the anchors to which Muslims looked for guidance. Close contact was also maintained with the other religious centers of Islam, e.g., Mecca and Medina, in Saudi Arabia.

At this time the popularity of *peers* (religious guides) was also developing among the Muslims. The *peers* resided in remote places away from the common people, but nonetheless they attracted people from far and wide. Their *dargahs* (mosques) attracted not only Muslims but non-Muslims as well. As a result of mass conversion of the local people to Islam, many local practices and even beliefs not allowed by orthodox Islam found their way into the Muslim society of Bengal. Many of the present-day rites and rituals obtaining among East Pakistan Muslims may be traced back to this period. Beliefs in numerous supernatural forces and the influence of the *ojha*s (sorcerers) originate probably from this amalgam of local beliefs with Muslim religious practices. These non-Islamic practices initiated a number of religious reformist movements among Muslims to rid the society of these local practices. The most famous of these nineteenth-century reformist movements was the Faraizi movement, started by Haji Shariatullah.

The black days of the Muslims of Bengal began with the loss of political power to the East India Company in the eighteenth century. In 1793, Lord Charles Cornwallis, governor general of India, introduced in Bengal the Permanent Settlement, through which Muslims not only lost their lands but also came under the influence of the Hindu *zamindars* (landlords), created through the Permanent Settlement. Muslim religious and educational institutions also lost their land grants, while the scholars were deprived of their stipends. The dissemination of Islam and the impact of Muslim culture in Bengal thus received their greatest setback. The influence of Hindu *zamindars* increased, and the many non-Islamic practices began to enter the fold of Muslim society with greater force and even official support. The British agents also helped in suppressing the Muslim forces by implicitly aiding the Hindu *zamindars* in their clashes with Muslim reformers.

Although the Muslims lost their political power and suffered humiliation at the hands of the British rulers and the Hindu *zamindars*, their influence on the local culture remained as ever. A clear manifestation of this influence may be seen in the Vaishnava movement by Chaitanya Dey, who attempted to introduce casteless society, mass worship, and brotherhood among his Hindu disciples. The Hindus also learned Persian, the court language, to gain state employment. The large number of Muslim terms, like *Sarkar, Qanungo, Majumdar, Mussadi,* and *Howladar,* adopted by the Hindus are also instances of the Muslim influence. These words linger in Hindu homes even today. Thus there are many indications of cultural exchange and even integration between Muslims and Hindus in the villages of East Pakistan. Similar indications might be seen in the villages of West Bengal in India. It is noteworthy, however, that in spite of the close links between the two communities, the Muslims remained a distinct group in their behavior and beliefs. They persisted in their fight with both the British and the Hindus to keep intact their way of life, the final manifestation of which was the emergence of the Dominion of Pakistan, in August, 1947 (Karim, 1965).

This brief history of the Muslim society of East Pakistan has been presented to provide the correct historical perspective for many of the observations made in the following pages. The many socioreligious institutions established by the Muslims became part of the general culture influencing not only the beliefs and values of the Muslims but also, to a great extent, those of the Hindus living in East Pakistan.

Villagers have been challenged further by the attempts of the Pakistan government to modernize their way of life; and while these efforts to modernize the traditional agrarian society of the village have not as yet been successful, they have set into motion a series of social changes that will affect that society most definitely. In order to bring about a healthy and constructive social change, much must be known about the culture of the people, the motivating forces and drives in their way of life, their attitudes and prejudices, their view of life and the universe, and the interrelation of these various elements of social behavior. Unfortunately, little systematic information about village life in East Pakistan is available.

Social scientists have developed a number of methodological tools for the study of rural societies. So far, "participant observation" has proved to be one of the most effective and fruitful. In participant observation the investigator lives with the people and observes their behavior in their day-to-day life. This method, of course, requires great skill in observation and insight into the methodological intricacies of social research. It has been the most favored technique with social anthropologists. A number of rural and tribal communities throughout the world have been studied with the help of this technique.

The observations in this book are based partly on participant observation and partly on the systematic use of a pretested and carefully prepared schedule. The study required a period of five months to prepare, pretest, and administer a 108-item interview schedule. In addition to the observation and the schedule, a group of the heads of village families, selected at random, were thoroughly interviewed about their childhood experiences and their recent past.

The details of the development of the interview schedule may be summarized as collecting and formulating a list of statements and questions about village life and culture in general, carefully and systematically formulating the relevant questions out of the detailed information collected for the purpose, and pretesting these questions on a group of villagers (not the respondents) for the final formulation of the interview schedule. The questions finally included in the schedule were administered in Bengali by a specially trained, college-educated village boy, who had been taught through lectures and role-playing techniques.

A study based on interview and questionnaires is often suspect in the eyes of rigid scientific methodologists. Much can be said both for and against the use of interviews and questionnaires as methods of scientific observation. There are in the literature of the social sciences a number of excellent defenses of these methods. In the case of this study it was found that a combination of the social research methods were suitable for the present population where the respondents would not welcome a too close, prolonged, and scientifically controlled experimentation with their way of life by white-collar outsiders.

This situation points up some of the difficulties likely to be faced by investigators in semiliterate societies like the one under discussion. I. T. Sanders, in "Research with Peasants in Underdeveloped Areas," has described these hazards, and I would like to add my own experiences in this connection. Some of these difficulties are inherent in the rural social structure of Pakistan; others are owing to historical and cultural forces that have impinged on the rural people in this part of the world over the past two centuries. These forces have helped to build up certain attitudes and defense mechanisms in the villagers that interfere with their frank and straightforward expression of opinions. Years of slavery and dependence on the government have also made them look askance on all efforts to influence them. They are incredulous of all altruistic claims, for they do not expect that anybody would sincerely be interested in their welfare. Foreign rule and the behavior of government agents during many decades have built up the image in their minds that the government officer is a symbol of the authority of the rulers.

Culturally, these people, particularly the Muslims, have always relied on God for succor in times of need and stress. They have faith in the supernatural, and would feel lost and insecure without this dependence and faith in God. They have a predominantly fatalistic attitude to change, believing that no human hand without the will of God can change anything. "Not a leaf moves without the will of God" is their fundamental approach to life. The villager's reliance on God, Fate, and the Unseen is much greater than on anything he comes across in his workaday life. Given such a social and cultural attitude to life, any attempt with whatever implicit or professed intentions is likely to meet with either resistance or indifference, both of which are not conducive to social investigation.

Closely related to the villager's fatalism are his attitudes towards the government programs and policies and its officers. His idea of the government remains fundamentally unchanged. He is suspicious of the intentions of the government change agents. He may be afraid that the research worker (associated with the government agent) is collecting information in order ultimately to increase his taxes or to seize his crop yield. He may even suspect that the field investigator is a member of some government agency. These and many other questions may arise in the mind of the villager at the sight of a person wanting some kind of information. In connection with natural disasters of all kinds, the government is looked upon as an agency for supplying relief. Under such circumstances the research investigator may be approached and even requested to communicate their demands for financial assistance to the government.

A third factor adding to the inherent difficulties of social research in the village is the value system embedded in the social structure. There is a fairly rigid hierarchy of leadership and of social roles in the village. The rich man or some responsible member of his family is always the one who should be approached for information about the village. A poor man would be violating the established social norm if he received an outsider and attempted to answer his questions about the village on his own instead of taking the visitor to the *sirdar* (leader) or to a *maatbar* (a prominent person) of the village.

Furthermore, the village leadership is still in the hands of the older generation in most of the villages of East Pakistan. An educated young man should, therefore, be very careful not to violate another social norm; namely, respect for age. It is categorical that no one could approach a village woman for conversation; she is inaccessible. She does not count as far as village affairs are concerned. Therefore, research interviews are out of the question. Even educated women investigators would be frowned upon.

In addition to these general features of the rural social structure, there are a number of specific difficulties that occurred during the course of the investigation in East Pakistan. These difficulties relate partly to the accuracy of the research data and partly to the investigator's personal conduct in the rural setting, and are recorded here for the benefit of Western readers in their understanding of village society in East Pakistan.

Villagers look at the government as an agency whose resources are unlimited, but in which they have no share. Because they believe they will receive government aid only in dire need, they tend to exaggerate their poverty and helplessness in order to invoke the pity and generosity of the government agents. Hence, data on the economic conditions collected from villagers, even after natural calamities, are not always accurate; and the investigator should employ other more reliable ways to cross-check information received from villagers. The value of information received from one group of villagers about another is also suspect.

Much of the villagers' cooperation with a government agent stems from fear of what will happen to them if they do not cooperate. They will never risk offending or antagonizing a government official, and because a white-collar investigator is readily associated with the government, all responses to an investigator's questions may be conditioned by the age-old attitude of the villagers. Nor will they immediately trust an investigator, who must devote much time to establish a relationship of trust and confidence with the village people. When they realize that an investigator is not a government agent, they may ignore him; for they realize that the investigator is neither in a position to help or to harm them. Whether from fear of a government agent or indifference to a social investigator, the data obtained from the villagers are necessarily limited in value.

There are certain areas of life villagers refuse to discuss; for example, women, sex relations, and aspects of family planning and contraception. The degree of animosity these topics would cause may vary from village to village; but, in general, one would receive a cold response, or none at all. Questions about their attitude towards the government in power would receive a similar response.

Villagers' interest in any visitor is maintained only as long as the visitor satisfies their curiosity about government loans, relief, and subsidies. Should the investigator admit his ignorance of these matters, the villagers will treat him as a nobody or as a liar, both of which positions are damaging to research. If, on the other hand, the investigator indicates that he is familiar with the procedures for obtaining government aid, he will be faced with requests and demands to help the villagers get it. At the same time, he is immediately associated with the government.

Difficulty in communication between the investigator and the people of the village is another element of which research workers should be aware. In many cases the investigator will be classed as belonging to a higher economic group than the villagers and given preferential treatment. For example, a fuss will be made about chairs and tables for the visitor. Many people may gather out of curiosity when the investigator arrives. In such a setting, frank and straightforward interviewing is hardly a practical proposition. Differences in speech can cause a problem. Even if the written language of the interviewer and the interviewee is the same, a great difference in their speech may cause a total lack of communication. Moreover, certain social science concepts, like "development," "change," "modern," and "urban," are difficult to translate in schedules prepared in the local language. Responses to one-word translations of these concepts are confusing and sometimes meaningless.

There is always a certain amount of resistance to an outsider in any community, but particularly in a village of East Pakistan, where the villagers do not trust a stranger, may resent him, and be uncommunicative. Unfortunately, the position of an educated investigator is always that of an outsider.

When an outsider enters a village, everyone is curious to know who he is, and he may soon have a crowd of from ten to fifty people around him. It is almost impossible to talk to a villager alone. Should the interviewer ask questions of one person, everyone in the crowd starts answering, or talking, and no one will appreciate the interviewer's desire to speak to a person privately. Even the person selected will be uneasy because he will fear the censure and suspicion of the other villagers after the investigator has left. It is also difficult to get responses to direct questions.

The moment an investigator asks for a specific person in the village, that person begins to wonder why of all the people available he has been chosen for the interview. He is not familiar with sampling techniques, and does not share the investigator's concern for the validity and reliability of information. Furthermore, even if he is available alone and is willing to be interviewed, it will not be possible for the semiliterate or almost illiterate villager to conform to the investigator's research plans. It is often difficult to keep the respondent talking to the point. The interviewer must be very patient, and be prepared to sort out relevant information from the entire conversation. For example, one should not expect a villager to answer questions with a categorical "yes" or "no."

Besides these specific problems and difficulties of social investigation, a point concerning the general methodology and the procedure of social research may also be noted. The investigator must always be ready to adjust his research design and field procedures to the demands of the situation, which, at times, may be most unexpected. Rigid methodological tools would not be workable.

Initially, I faced these difficulties in my investigation; but as it progressed, most of them were overcome, especially because the institution I represented was held in great esteem by the villagers. There was no great difficulty in establishing a rapport with them, and I was not treated either as an outsider or as a government agent. There was, however, the initial difficulty of communication, and I had to show my awareness of the taboos of village life.

There are various levels of analysis for the study of any society. The problems of a society can be analyzed in terms of its social structure, values and beliefs, and the power structure of its various hierarchies, or merely in terms of its economy and the methods of production, consumption, and marketing. Another aspect of the analysis may only relate to the political climate, bases, and the dynamics of the sociopolitical structure. For a comprehensive analysis of any society, therefore, all the various levels of analysis should be presented, although in these days of specialization it is hardly feasible or possible for any one individual to present competently such an analysis.

This book attempts to describe in a systematic but general way the sociopsychological and sociological problems of East Pakistan rural society. It is neither the purpose nor the claim here to cover the political and economic aspects of these problems. It may, however, be added that whenever necessary and possible, the political and economic aspects of the society under study will be touched upon to explain the social-psychological behavior of the people. It is also expected that a social-psychological analysis of the problems will often throw light on the economic and political behavior of the people.

Although limited in its scope because of the sharp and narrow specialties in the social sciences today, I shall attempt to present as broad-based a picture of East Pakistan village culture as possible. It is my contention, however, that an interdisciplinary team of authorities should take up studies of the various aspects of the East Pakistan society, whereby scholars from different social sciences contribute their knowledge in the analysis of a changing society.

The research reported in these pages specifically relates to a social-psychological survey of two villages in the district of Comilla, East Pakistan. One of the two villages, which we shall call Ramnagar, was populated entirely by Muslims. The other village, which we shall call Alipur, had both Muslim and Hindu families. For the survey, 50 per cent of all the heads of Muslim families in the two villages were chosen at random. Since the Hindu families were about one-third of the total number of Muslim families, all the available heads of families were selected for this survey. There were thus ninety-four Muslim and fifty-five Hindu respondents in the sample. The counting of the families was done through personal checking from door to door in each village. Prior to the final question-naire, a brief survey of the economic and material possessions of the village families was taken. This survey gave me the background information on the literacy, furniture and utensils in each house, landed property of the family, ornaments, books, and other such material possessions of the people in these two villages. After the interviewees for the final survey were selected, the remaining heads of families (Muslims only) were used for the pretesting of the research instrument.

A word about the representativeness of these villages in the context of East Pakistan rural society. The two villages under study are located near a district town (population about 40,000) and by the side of a *pucca* road and, therefore, are not inaccessible to outsiders. These two features—that is, acces-sibility and nearness to a semiurban population—set these villages apart because not many villages in riverine East Pakistan have these two facilities. The choice of these two villages for the investigation was made precisely for these reasons, with the implicit assumption that, for the type of study being made, the villages were fairly typical of East

Pakistan village culture. Culturally, all villages in East Pakistan
are more or less uniform. In terms of the attitudes and beliefs,
usages and customs, even towns like the district town are
similar to the villages. The mofussil towns are still far from
being urbanized; therefore, there would be no basis for assum-
ing that the villagers in our sample were urbanized or influenced
by their nearness to the town. In respect to the psychological
characteristics, basic motivations and values, and even personality, our respondents are fairly typical of East Pakistani villagers.

# CHAPTER II

# LIFE IN THE VILLAGES

EAST PAKISTAN is a part of the Assam-Bengal belt. It still retains its beauty, natural simplicity, and rugged charms although the economic solvency and the financial stability of its people have suffered greatly through the years. Centuries ago when Ibn Batuttah traveled by boat from Sylhet to Sonargaon he noted water wheels, gardens, and villages on both sides of the Brahamputra River (Rahim, 1963). He sailed through villages and gardens that impressed him with their lush, green paddy fields and fruit-laden trees. This was Bengal's rural scene in A.D. 1345. Even today the traveler through various parts of East Pakistan cannot but be impressed by the sad beauty and almost primitive sites he will pass.

Villages in East Pakistan still abound in fruit trees, water tanks, and paddy fields. Traveling by air, boat, or train one notes small clusters of hamlets surrounded by banana, jack fruit, and palm trees. There are mango groves, and hidden behind these tall, thick trees are the thatched walls and tin and thatched roofs in which 95 per cent of the population of East Pakistan live. The simple villagers earn their meager subsistence partly through cultivation of small holdings, and partly through other less lucrative subsidiary occupations like selling milk, fishing, handicrafts, and manual labor.

Agriculture and fishing are the two stable occupations of the East Pakistani villagers. Since agriculture, because of the primitive methods employed does not keep them busy throughout the year, they either sit idle or engage in subsidiary occupations, which are usually of a casual nature. Fishing is both a pastime and a necessary supplement of food and income. There is a class of fishermen who spend most of their lives in small, country boats and catch fish for a living. It is sad to see them risking their lives through cyclones and floods; but it is definitely a pleasure to sail with them during the dry season and see them casting their nets. Rivers near Dacca and Narayanganj attract many fishermen in small boats who can earn extra money from visitors wanting to enjoy a boat ride on the river.

A village in East Pakistan is a picturesque scene in spite of the dire poverty of the inhabitants. Most villages abound in water resources, although the irony of the situation is that one of the biggest agricultural problems of East Pakistan is the scarcity of water—not for lack of water, but because of the absence of facilities for holding or preserving water. The village tanks remain dry for part of the year.

An East Pakistan village is relatively small in comparison to a village of West Pakistan, the average size being about 500 persons and the average cultivated area about 100 acres. Every village has a few landless families subsisting on part-time labor during sowing and harvesting seasons. There may be three or four families owning 10 to 12 acres of land each, and about 50 per cent of the families owning about 1 to 3 acres of agricultural land each. The average family of six in the Comilla district owns 1.7 acres of land.

Communication in East Pakistan is generally difficult and time-consuming. Most of the villages are inaccessible by road transport. During the rainy season many of them are submerged or surrounded by water, and are accessible only by small country boats. Except for those villages located by the side of a road or near a district and divisional headquarters, they are always inaccessible except on foot.

There is generally a market (*haat*) serving about one dozen villages. These *haat*s are held once or twice a week, and serve as the meeting place for persons from neighboring villages. People bring their marketable articles to sell, and take home items for consumption. *Haat*s serve both social and economic needs of the people, and sometime become venues for cultural and political activities.

In the village one can meet people either in the field or under trees or in some centrally located places, gossiping and idling away. The conversation mostly relates to the immediate interests of the people. There is a frequent mention of present poverty, past plenty, government relief, and the village factions in which they may personally be involved. There are discussions about the difficulties of village life and the lack of facilities for agricultural seeds and fertilizers. In their conversation one can sense the basic insecurity plaguing the life of a villager. A very clear picture of village problems can be obtained from their comments.

Most villages have some sort of elementary school and one or two mosques. The school is generally a *madrasah*, where the Holy Qur'ān is taught to small boys and girls. The village teacher and the *imam* (person who leads the congregation) of the mosque are the prominent persons besides the *sirdar*s and the *maatbar*s. The people listen to them and, in general, accept their advice. They are respected, and constitute a force and very often a barrier to be reckoned with in matters of social and economic change. Their influence is undoubtedly waning because more informed channels of information through the young, educated boys and the government change agents are now available (Rahim, 1965). However, in matters other than agricultural and particularly in religion, family planning, and the use of scientific medicine, the *imam* and the teacher are still a strong force of resistance.

The villages are divided into two or more *para*s (sections), either on a geographical basis or on the basis of kinship locations. Sometimes there may be another basis of social relationship whereby certain *bari*s (families with equal status and similar background, though not necessarily related by blood) are contiguously located. In every village there are a few prominent families that have for decades guided village politics. These families are generally known by the surname or professional designations of their heads. Thus there are *Deputy bari, Muktar bari, Munshi bari, Majumdar bari, Hadji bari,* and *Chowdhary bari.* There may also be a *Nawab bari* or *Zamindar bari* in certain villages.

Another feature of the East Pakistan village is the pattern of its leadership. There is generally an informal council of elders whose members are variously known as *sirdars* and *maatbars*. The position is normally inherited by the oldest son from the family head, and the villagers have traditionally been accepting this transfer of leadership. In the past this group of elders exercised informally many functions of the judiciary. They still prescribe social controls in the village. It may be noted, however, that the *sirdari* system is slowly dying out as a result of various modernizing influences that have recently entered the village. Another factor responsible for weakening the solidarity of village leadership is the presence of numerous factions in the villages. These factions have very complicated dimensions, and will be discussed in a separate chapter. Suffice it to say here that the various factions are an important aspect of rural social organization in East Pakistan. However, in many respects, they are similar to those factions obtaining and reported from most parts of the Pak-Indian subcontinent (Lewis, 1954; Inayatullah, 1958).

With this general profile of East Pakistan village life, we now present the socioeconomic features of the two villages under investigation, along with case studies of some village farmers by way of introduction to our respondents and their problems.

## RAMNAGAR

Ramnagar is a small village with a population of 506 persons, including both males and females. Table 1 gives the population distribution. The number of males is 23 more than the females. This sex ratio, however, may not be general in East Pakistan. The age distribution in Ramnagar is also disproportionate. A little over half the population are below 20 years of age, 5 per cent are over 65 years of age, and the oldest man is over 100 years old.

Ramnagar has one landless family. The other families have differing sizes of landholdings. Tables 2 and 3, respectively, give the sizes of the family and the landholdings. It can be

TABLE 1

Age and Sex Distributions of the Population in the Two Villages

| Age Range (years) | Ramnagar | | Alipur | |
|---|---|---|---|---|
| | Male | Female | Male | Female |
| 0 – 4 | 37 | 35 | 71 | 65 |
| 5 – 9 | 49 | 42 | 81 | 84 |
| 10 – 14 | 30 | 27 | 62 | 45 |
| 15 – 19 | 20 | 17 | 38 | 27 |
| 20 – 24 | 13 | 17 | 37 | 22 |
| 25 – 29 | 24 | 12 | 36 | 37 |
| 30 – 34 | 10 | 19 | 25 | 33 |
| 35 – 39 | 10 | 21 | 29 | 34 |
| 40 – 44 | 17 | 12 | 26 | 19 |
| 45 – 49 | 16 | 11 | 16 | 16 |
| 50 – 54 | 13 | 8 | 15 | 12 |
| 55 – 59 | 6 | 5 | 9 | 10 |
| 60 – 64 | 10 | 2 | 14 | 11 |
| 65 – 69 | 2 | 3 | 13 | 3 |
| 70 – 74 | 5 | 6 | 1 | 8 |
| 75 – 79 | 1 | 2 | 2 | 3 |
| 80 – 84 | 0 | 2 | 2 | 1 |
| 85 – 89* | 1 | 0 | 0 | 3 |
| | 264 | 241 | 477 | 433 |

* One man each in Ramnagar and Alipur is above one hundred years of age.

TABLE 2

Size of Families in the Two Villages

| Number of Persons 666 | Number and Per Cent of Families | | | |
|---|---|---|---|---|
| | Ramnagar | | Alipur | |
| | Number | Per Cent* | Number | Per Cent |
| 1 | 3 | 3 | 6 | 4 |
| 2 | 7 | 8 | 13 | 8 |
| 3 | 11 | 12 | 21 | 12 |
| 4 | 12 | 13 | 25 | 15 |
| 5 | 11 | 12 | 29 | 17 |
| 6 | 19 | 21 | 27 | 16 |
| 7 | 10 | 11 | 23 | 13 |
| 8 | 5 | 6 | 11 | 6 |
| 9 | 6 | 7 | 6 | 4 |
| 10 | 0 | 0 | 6 | 4 |
| 11 | 2 | 2 | 2 | 1 |
| 12 | 1 | 1 | 2 | 1 |
| 13 | 1 | 1 | 0 | 0 |
| 14 | 2 | 2 | 0 | 0 |
| | 90 | | 171 | |

* Fractions have been rounded off to the nearest whole number in calculating the percentages.

TABLE 3

Size of Landholding per Family in the Two Villages

| Landholding (in acres) | Number and Per Cent of Families | | | |
| | Ramnagar | | Alipur | |
| | Number | Per Cent* | Number | Per Cent |
|---|---|---|---|---|
| Less than 1 | 15 | 17 | 63 | 37 |
| 1 but less than 2 | 16 | 18 | 50 | 29 |
| 2 but less than 3 | 21 | 23 | 21 | 12 |
| 3 but less than 4 | 12 | 13 | 12 | 7 |
| 4 but less than 5 | 5 | 6 | 11 | 6 |
| 5 but less than 6 | 3 | 3 | 1 | 1 |
| 6 but less than 7 | 9 | 10 | 4 | 2 |
| 7 but less than 8 | 0 | 0 | 3 | 2 |
| 8 but less than 9 | 2 | 2 | 1 | 1 |
| 9 but less than 10 | 0 | 0 | 1 | 1 |
| 10 but less than 11 | 4 | 4 | 0 | 0 |
| 11 but less than 12 | 0 | 0 | 0 | 0 |
| 12 but less than 13 | 2 | 2 | 0 | 0 |
| | 89 | | 167 | |

Note: One family in Ramnagar and four families in Alipur have no land.

* Fractions have been rounded off to the nearest whole number in calculating the percentages.

TABLE 4

Type and Number of Houses in the Two Villages

| Type of Houses | Number and Per Cent of Houses | | | |
| | Ramnagar | | Alipur | |
| | Number | Per Cent* | Number | Per Cent |
|---|---|---|---|---|
| A. Bamboo wall and thatched roof | 91 | 54 | 129 | 43 |
| B. Mud wall and thatched roof | 50 | 29 | 106 | 35 |
| C. Mud wall and metal†roof | 14 | 8 | 18 | 6 |
| D. Bamboo wall and metal roof | 13 | 8 | 27 | 9 |
| E. Tin wall and tin roof | 1 | 1 | 9 | 3 |
| F. Brick wall and metal roof | 1 | 1 | 9 | 3 |
| G. Brick wall and thatched roof | 0 | 0 | 1 | 0 |
| | 170 | | 299 | |

* Fractions have been rounded off to the nearest whole number in calculating percentages.

†Metal refers to corrugated iron (C.I.) sheets used for roofing.

TABLE 5
Number of persons in the Two Villages Who Have Attended School (Primary and English)

| Level of Schooling | Number of Persons (Primary) | | Number of Persons (English) | |
|---|---|---|---|---|
| | Ramnagar | Alipur | Ramnagar | Alipur |
| Up to Class 1 | 35 | 122 | 0 | 0 |
| Up to Class 2 | 18 | 61 | 0 | ʊ |
| Up to Class 3 | 10 | 88 | 0 | 21 |
| Up to Class 4 | 10 | 36 | 0 | 0 |
| Up to Class 5 | 8 | 21 | 0 | 0 |
| Up to Class 6 | 0 | 0 | 6 | 13 |
| Up to Class 7 | 0 | 0 | 3 | 9 |
| Up to Class 8 | 0 | 0 | 6 | 1 |
| Up to Class 9 | 0 | 0 | 2 | 8 |
| Up to Class 10 | 0 | 0 | 2 | 7 |
| Matriculates* | 0 | 0 | 4 | 5 |

* Twenty-three persons in Ramnagar have attended *madrasah* to learn the Holy Qur'ān. Among the matriculates in Alipur, one person received training for primary teachers, and two have a national certificate of medicine. Besides, there is one *maulvi* with a certificate from a religious school, and one Hindu teacher with training (*guru* training) in the Hindu system of schooling. Matriculation is equal to higher secondary, after which two years' schooling is required to enter the University at the B.A. level.

seen that fifty-two families have less than three acres each, and only twenty families have a landholding above five acres each. Economically, therefore, only 12 per cent of the villagers can be sustained on the family land. The remaining 88 per cent either starve part of the year or get in debt and ultimately sell away whatever little land they have. As if this situation were not bad enough, sixty-three families in Ramnagar have from four to nine members, all of whom draw their sustenance from the family land. Six families in the village have fourteen members each.

There are ninety family kitchens in Ramnagar, which has a total of 170 huts, including the shelters for cattle that are contiguous to the family living quarters. Table 4 gives the details of their structure. Most of these huts contain only one room. The majority of them have bamboo walls and thatched roofs, but many have mud walls. There are 28 houses with metal roofs, generally of corrugated iron sheets. Only 1 house in Ramnagar has brick walls. Another has both the walls and the roof made of tin.

From a most liberal definition of literacy, Ramnagar has 110 literate persons in a population of 506 persons. Table 5 gives the details of the literacy in this village. The percentage is about the same as for the whole of East Pakistan (21 per cent). However, if we eliminate those below five years of age, the rate of literacy goes up to 25 per cent.

The general poverty of the village homes should already be apparent. As seen in Table 6, not many people have a bed to sleep on. Fifty-two per cent of the families have at least one *chowki* (wooden bed) in the house, out of which only 20 per cent have more than one. Other members of the family sleep on bamboo mats spread on the floor. Fifteen families have at least one table, and twenty have one chair each in the house. These items are meant for occasional visitors in the village. The same families also have one wooden stool each in the house. This is about all the furniture in the village. (See the Appendix for a list of articles obtainable in an average village house. The list, though long, would not exceed 100 rupees in value.)

TABLE 6
Number and Type of Furniture in the Village Houses

| Number* of Articles | Tables Ram-nagar | Alipur | Chairs Ram-nagar | Alipur | Almirahs Ram-nagar | Alipur | Stool Ram-nagar | Alipur | Chowkis Ram-nagar | Alipur |
|---|---|---|---|---|---|---|---|---|---|---|
| 0 | 75 | 125 | 70 | 120 | 77 | 130 | 65 | 111 | 43 | 84 |
| 1 | 13 | 35 | 13 | 30 | 12 | 31 | 19 | 44 | 29 | 58 |
| 2 | 0 | 10 | 7 | 9 | 1 | 6 | 5 | 11 | 12 | 13 |
| 3 | 2 | 0 | 0 | 8 | 0 | 1 | 0 | 1 | 5 | 5 |
| 4 | 0 | 1 | 0 | 2 | 0 | 2 | 1 | 3 | 1 | 8 |
| 5 | 0 | 0 | 0 | 1 | 0 | 1 | 0 | 0 | 0 | 2 |
| 6 | 0 | 0 | 0 | 1 | 0 | 0 | 0 | 1 | 0 | 1 |
| | 90 | 171 | 90 | 171 | 90 | 171 | 90 | 171 | 90 | 171 |

* Eighty-six out of 90 families in Ramnagar, and 158 out of 171 families in Alipur have some items of indigenous furniture like *moras, piris*, trunks, boxes of wood, and other things made of bamboo and cane.

TABLE 7

Number of Families in the Two Villages Possessing Ornaments
Made of Gold, Silver, and Rolled Gold*

| Weight (in tolas) | Number of Families | | | | | |
|---|---|---|---|---|---|---|
| | Gold | | Silver | | Rolled Gold | |
| | Ram-nagar | Alipur | Ram-nagar | Alipur | Ram-nagar | Alipur |
| 0 | 45 | 83 | 66 | 104 | 90 | 163 |
| Less than 1 | 37 | 42 | 0 | 17 | 0 | 4 |
| 1 but less than 2 | 4 | 24 | 13 | 20 | 0 | 3 |
| 2 but less than 3 | 1 | 13 | 8 | 12 | 0 | 0 |
| 3 but less than 4 | 2 | 4 | 2 | 8 | 0 | 1 |
| 4 but less than 5 | 0 | 2 | 1 | 3 | 0 | 0 |
| 5 but less than 6 | 1 | 2 | 0 | 0 | 0 | 0 |
| 6 but less than 7 | 0 | 0 | 0 | 2 | 0 | 0 |
| 7 but less than 8 | 0 | 0 | 0 | 2 | 0 | 0 |
| 8 but less than 9 | 0 | 0 | 0 | 1 | 0 | 0 |
| | 90 | 170 | 90 | 169 | 90 | 171 |

* In Alipur one family has more than ten *tola*s of gold and another, more than
twelve *tola*s of silver. One family has about five pounds of silver. One *tola* is equal
to about one-fortieth of a pound in weight.

Surveys in West Pakistan have indicated that the villagers
put greater premium on ornaments than on cash. In Ramnagar
also, in spite of their poverty, whenever possible village girls
and women try to own ornaments. As shown in Table 7,
thirty-seven families in Ramnagar have less than one *tola* of
gold, forty-five families have no gold at all, and three have
between four and six *tola*s each. Twenty-four families also have
some silver ornaments.

The majority of the households in Ramnagar use earthen
utensils for cooking and eating. Many families have as many
as thirty earthen pots in the house. Some families have a few
utensils made of aluminum, china, copper, tin, and iron (see
Table 8).

The number and kind of books in each household are
given in Table 9. Forty-three families have from one to four
religious books; ten have from one to four Bengali novels, and
one family has ten novels. Three families also have *Puthi*
literature in the house. A number of families have textbooks
belonging to school- and college-going children.

TABLE 8

Number and Make of Utensils in the Families* of the Two Villages

| Number of Items | Number of Families Possessing Utensils of Different Metals in Ramnagar and Alipur | | | | | | | | | | | |
|---|---|---|---|---|---|---|---|---|---|---|---|---|
| | Earthen | | Aluminum | | China | | Tin | | Copper | | Iron | |
| | R. | A. | R. | A. | R. | A. | R. | A. | R. | A. | R. | A. |
| 0 | 3 | 10 | 11 | 15 | 20 | 68 | 58 | 54 | 24 | 37 | 60 | 81 |
| 1 to 3 | 0 | 0 | 36 | 59 | 38 | 57 | 22 | 86 | 45 | 88 | 25 | 81 |
| 4 to 6 | 1 | 9 | 23 | 76 | 20 | 28 | 8 | 24 | 21 | 23 | 0 | 4 |
| 7 to 9 | 4 | 11 | 8 | 11 | 5 | 11 | 0 | 4 | 0 | 11 | 5 | 2 |
| 10 to 12 | 7 | 35 | 10 | 8 | 5 | 3 | 1 | 2 | 0 | 7 | 0 | 3 |
| 13 to 15 | 15 | 26 | 2 | 2 | 1 | 0 | 0 | 0 | 0 | 0 | 0 | 0 |
| 16 to 18 | 4 | 10 | 0 | 0 | 1 | 2 | 1 | 0 | 0 | 1 | 0 | 0 |
| 19 to 21 | 11 | 31 | 0 | 0 | 0 | 0 | 0 | 1 | 0 | 1 | 0 | 0 |
| 22 to 24 | 2 | 2 | 0 | 0 | 0 | 1 | 0 | 0 | 0 | 0 | 0 | 0 |
| 25 to 27 | 17 | 26 | 0 | 0 | 0 | 0 | 0 | 0 | 0 | 3 | 0 | 0 |
| 28 to 30 | 26 | 11 | 0 | 0 | 0 | 0 | 0 | 0 | 0 | 0 | 0 | 0 |

* In Alipur nine families have more than forty earthen pots, and one family each has more than forty china and copper utensils.

TABLE 9

Number and Type of Books in Families in the Two Villages*

| Number of Books | Number of Families Having Different Types of Books | | | | | | | |
|---|---|---|---|---|---|---|---|---|
| | Religious | | Novels | | Folk Literature | | Textbooks | |
| | Ramnagar | Alipur | Ramnagar | Alipur | Ramnagar | Alipur | Ramnagar | Alipur |
| 0 | 47 | 80 | 79 | 153 | 87 | 166 | 66 | 112 |
| 1 | 40 | 60 | 4 | 3 | 1 | 0 | 3 | 8 |
| 2 | 2 | 16 | 2 | 6 | 1 | 3 | 1 | 3 |
| 3 | 0 | 6 | 2 | 3 | 1 | 0 | 4 | 13 |
| 4 | 1 | 2 | 2 | 1 | 0 | 0 | 9 | 9 |
| 5 | 0 | 4 | 0 | 0 | 0 | 0 | 0 | 10 |
| 6 | 0 | 1 | 0 | 0 | 0 | 0 | 1 | 8 |
| 7 | 0 | 0 | 0 | 0 | 0 | 2 | 0 | 2 |
| 8 | 0 | 0 | 0 | 1 | 0 | 0 | 2 | 2 |
| 9 | 0 | 0 | 0 | 0 | 0 | 0 | 2 | 0 |
| 10 | 0 | 0 | 1 | 2 | 0 | 0 | 2 | 4 |

* In addition, two families in Alipur have fifteen novels and fifteen religious books.

Reference has already been made to the modernizing influences from outside. The impact of such influences can be seen in the villages near urban or semiurban towns in terms of the villagers' desire to possess modern amenities of life. Our survey of Ramnagar's socioeconomic life indicated that fourteen families have their own bicycles, three families have wrist watches, and one family has a wall clock. Eighteen families have fountain pens, out of which one family has two· and three families have three fountain pens each.

This general profile of Ramnagar suggests that in physical features, in the general socioeconomic level, type and size of houses, and the size and landholdings of families, it is like any other village in East Pakistan. The village is, however, atypical in respect to communication because one can reach Ramnagar by motor vehicle, which is not true for most of the villages in East Pakistan. In terms of the general level of literacy and awareness of modern amenities, the village may be better off than most. In all other respects, and especially in respect to the difficulties of living, beliefs and attitudes, and general adjustment to the vagaries of nature, the village is thought to be quite typical of the East Pakistan rural scene.

## ALIPUR

There are 171 families in Alipur, out of which 40 per cent are Hindus, whose main occupations are·weaving and farming. Among the Muslims the majority are farmers who sell milk and engage in casual labor as a subsidiary occupation. The village is divided into three *para*s, each of which is large enough to be designated a village itself.

There are 911 persons in Alipur, out of which 47 per cent are females. Forty-five per cent of the total population of Alipur are below fourteen years of age, and only 7 per cent are above sixty years of age. The size of an average family in Alipur is 4, which is less than the average for other East Pakistan villages. One reason for the small size of the family in this village may be the fact that in many Hindu families some members have migrated to India after Independence, thus reducing the size of the average family for the entire village.

With agriculture being the main occupation, the entire village is engaged in cultivation. The size of the landholdings is small. Out of 171 families, 113 have less than two acres to subsist on. Even the best methods of agriculture could hardly make these holdings adequate. It has been found that the lowest measure of land to be economically viable in East Pakistan should be five acres per family. In terms of economic viability, therefore, only 10 families in Alipur have the necessary land to live on. There are also 4 landless families in Alipur.

The pattern of housing in Alipur is similar to that in other East Pakistan villages. In Table 4 we find that out of 299 housing units, 156 have bamboo walls and metal or thatched roofs; and 124 have mud walls and metal or thatched roofs. Ten houses have brick walls, 9 with metal roofs and 1 thatched. Nine other houses have both the walls and the roofs made of tin.

The literacy percentage for Alipur is higher than that of other villages. Because Hindu families have more education, literacy has gone up to 43 per cent of all villagers over the age of five. This group includes five college-educated persons. Besides, one person has had normal school training for primary teachers. There are two medical practitioners, one Hindu and one Muslim, with a national certificate for medicine. Both of these practitioners are leaders of their communities, and are deeply involved with the village factions and politics.

There are more books in this village than in Ramnagar. Sixteen families have an average of about four Bengali novels each. Five families have *Puthi* literature, and eighty-nine have an average of two religious books. Two families have an average of two religious books. Two families have fifteen novels and fifteen religious books. One of these religious books is the Holy Qur'ān, or *Gita*. Fifty-nine families have school- or college-going children, and have a number of textbooks in the house. The Muslim households have more books on religion than the Hindu households.

In terms of utensils and furniture, Alipur also rates above the average village in East Pakistan. More than 30 families

have one chair and one table each. The same families also
have an *almirah* and stools. However, about 50 per cent of the
families have one *chowki* to sleep on. Some families have up to
six *chowki*s, almost one for each member of the family. Besides,
158 families in Alipur have utility items like *mora*s (stools),
*piri*s (plank seats), boxes, and steel trunks. The utensils in
most of the households are earthen, but the fact that at least
57 families use china, copper, and aluminum wares indicates
that the villagers do not like to use earthen wares, and use
them only because they cannot afford to buy better things.
China and copper utensils are indicators of social status in
the village. The most common utensils used in the households
are made of copper, aluminum, tin, and iron, with china as
the most preferred.

Gold ornaments are a valuable possession even in urban
communities, but the villagers put particular emphasis on the
possession of gold by the family. The next in value is silver, but
only as a very poor substitute for gold. In Alipur, eighty-seven
families have gold ornaments, out of which forty-five have more
than one *tola* each, twenty-one have more than two *tola*s each,
two have up to five *tola*s each, and one family has more than
ten *tola*s of gold. Silver ornaments, whose weight varies from
one to eight *tola*s, were also reported to be owned by sixty-five
families.

Alipur, in general, is economically better off than Ramnagar, and can claim to have better social and cultural amenities.
There is a night school for adults, a *madrasah* for religious
instruction, two mosques, and two market places. There is also
a youth club organized by the Hindu weavers.

The following life histories, based on personal interviews
with some of the village people, will serve as mirrors in which
the problems and difficulties, joys and sorrows, tensions and
frustrations of the East Pakistan villagers are reflected.

*Abdur Rahman.* According to his own estimate, Rahman
is sixty-five years old. In general, estimates of time are always
inaccurate since there are no birth records, and a villager
calculates time in terms of certain important events in his
life. For example, Rahman's father, Lashkar Gazi, died about

twenty years ago. His father had married thrice; first, at the age of eighteen; and after the death of his first wife, a second time, at the age of twenty-five. The third marriage, after the death of his second wife, took place at the age of forty. Lashkar Gazi had five sons. One of the peculiarities of this family, as told by Rahman, is that for the last two generations there has been no female issue.

This family's only occupation is farming. Lashkar Gazi originally possessed five *kanis* (about two acres) of land. He sold half of it to pay his debts to the moneylender. Abdur Rahman and his brothers lived separately during the life of their father. Abdur Rahman is the youngest son of his father by his third wife. His four brothers were born of the first and second wives, two from each. The brothers lived harmoniously. Three stepbrothers of Rahman are dead, and the one living stays with his maternal uncle whose daughter he married. Abdur Rahman is thus the only surviving member of the family living in this village.

Abdur Rahman is illiterate, and because the small portion of land he inherited from his father is quite insufficient to support his family, he works as a laborer.

Recalling his childhood days, Rahman said that the Hindus were wealthier and belonged to two subcastes, *Ghosh* and *Tanti* (milkmen and weavers). There were many moneylenders among the Hindus. The Muslims in the village were poor, but the reason for their poverty was the presence of these unscrupulous moneylenders who sucked their blood. The Muslims were mainly unlettered farmers while the Hindus, though not highly educated, were fairly literate. About 400 people lived in the village then out of which about 30 per cent were Hindus.

Nothing spectacular happened in Rahman's childhood, except when the Gumti River flooded about four miles away from his village. The flood caused terrible damage to the crops and many heads of cattle were swept away. Abdur Rahman, along with the other members of his family and many of the villagers, took shelter on a hillock near the village. They remained there for about a fortnight. The government gave them rice for only a couple of days. That critical situation was one the entire village had to face. It may be a typical childhood experience for many villagers of East Pakistan.

Among the Muslims, Abdur Rahman recalls, were two renowned families, namely, the *Qazi* and *Munshi bari*s known for their aristocracy and culture. But now both these families have fallen on evil days. One of the members of these families is a village *maatbar*. Rahman feels that people were better off economically during his childhood. There were less mouths to feed, the cost of living was low, and the village was more or less self-sufficient. The Muslims, though less educated then, were more religious in their behavior. There was a *maulvi* in the *Qazi bari* who was the religious guide for the village.

Abdur Rahman has two sons and three daughters. The daughters have been given in marriage in nearby villages. One of his sons, who was an electrician, died two years ago. His older son, who is now thirty-three, has been married for twelve years, but has no children. This son served in the army for seven years, and was also an Ansar (a semimilitary voluntary organization in East Pakistan) for three years. Now he lives in the village and looks after the household. Abdur Rahman cannot undertake hard labor now; but he tries to help in marketing, feeding the cow, and washing clothes. There are only four persons in the family, but the land does not yield enough to feed them. The floods and the overflow of the Gumti embankment cause devastation to his crops. He is in very straitened circumstances economically; and complains that, in spite of the best efforts of the government, the cost of daily necessities is steeply rising.

Abdur Rahman is a cordial and amiable villager. He is an ordinary member of the rural community, although as an elderly member he has his opinions on the general economic situation of the village. He is unhappy about the increase of taxes by the Union Council. He is not opposed to certain socioeconomic changes in the village, but he feels that the people would accept changes if it were made clear that the changes would be beneficial to them. He is even willing to accept cooperative mechanized farming on a crop-sharing basis if it increases the yield of the land. He perceives most of the recent changes in agriculture in terms of their benefit to the economy of the village, and has arrived at the solution in terms of his own needs and deprivations, which are primarily economic at present.

In Abdur Rahman's life, as in the life of the other villagers, certain occasions are important and sacred. In East Pakistan these occasions are the harvesting season and the first eating of the new rice. Abdur Rahman also joins in these celebrations. He is superstitious, and would prefer not to start on a journey or begin a new plan on certain days and dates. He also considers it a bad omen if the cock crows at night or if a certain bird, called the "kali," crows near his house. Important religious occasions for Rahman are the two *Eid* festivals for Muslims (one after the month of fasting and the other on the occasion of *Hajj*, the pilgrimage to Mecca). Formerly the villagers also used to participate in the celebrations of *Jarigan* and *Jatra*, but now these celebrations are on the wane.

Abdur Rahman believes in God, and is highly religious in his attitude to life. For his difficulties and frustrations, he blames his luck. He does not agree that he can improve his situation with his own efforts. Everything is destined, and destiny cannot be changed. Even so, he thinks the government should help the people all it can because they can do nothing without it.

*Suraj Mia.* Suraj Mia, a man of fifty, is the head of his family. He had one stepbrother and seven sisters who, during the lifetime of his father, lived together. His stepbrother died about thirty years ago, leaving behind a son. Among the sisters, five got married during his father's lifetime and the other two were given in marriage by him. His father had fourteen *kanis* (5.6 acres) of land.

The village during Suraj's childhood was quite prosperous. People had enough to eat and were, for the most part, free from the worries of today. The cowsheds had healthy cattle, granaries were full of rice and paddy, and the tanks were full of fish. There were plenty of fruits and vegetables in the village. Suraj Mia recalls that once during his childhood the river embankment gave way and his and all the surrounding villages were flooded, their crops were destroyed, and their cattle were killed. Government agencies came with relief supplies to curb the famine that resulted. Tempers flared and there was a bloody quarrel between two factions of the village. An epidemic of cholera broke out, lasted six months, and killed hundreds of people.

Suraj Mia only went to the third class in the village primary school. He could not continue after the death of his stepbrother, for his father was growing old and needed him to take over the responsibility of providing for the family. He began working his land, and was happy.

Suraj married but once, thirty years ago, and had eight sons and three daughters. Three of the sons and one daughter died at an early age. His oldest son does the farming, and is not yet married. Like Suraj, this son had to leave school to help on the farm. His next son is in school, and his other two sons are in the village primary school. The two daughters of Suraj Mia are still minors.

Poverty and misery began for Suraj upon the death of his father, when he had to start providing for his family of nine with only half of the family land (seven *kanis*), the other half having gone to the son of his stepbrother. About twelve years ago there was another devastating flood, in which the crops were washed away and the mud walls of his house were demolished. Prices of rice went up to fifty rupees (about $11.00) a *maund* (eighty-two pounds). The family suffered greatly, and Suraj had to sell one *kani* of his land to buy food.

With only six *kanis* of land left, Suraj Mia supplements his income by selling milk and green vegetables produced in his fields. He feels that he can feed his family adequately and even educate his sons if the recurrent floods do not destroy his crops. He is happy when he gets a good crop; he is happier still when he has food grains stored in his own house. He seems to need nothing else from life to be content.

There is a perennial canal known as Kakri Gang running near the village. An embankment raised by the people of two villages protected last year's crops. This year the people in the neighboring villages quarreled among themselves, and one party cut the embankment, causing a flood and destruction of the crops.

Suraj Mia, who is a village *maatbar* and thereby associated with all the social and political activities of the village, is respected by everyone. He was happy with the old union boards under the local self government, but under the union councils (basic democracy) the taxes have been raised and the land revenue has gone up from 44 per cent to 50 per cent. Again if it cannot be paid at the proper time, interest is added to it, which was not done before the *zamindari* system was abolished. He has heard the rumor that new taxes on cattle, poultry, and boats are being proposed by the union councils. According to Suraj Mia, members of the union councils are not honest. All of them are corruptible, and one must offer a bribe even when applying for a loan.

Suraj Mia believes that all natural calamities are from God and, therefore, unavoidable. Of course, one can probably protect oneself from floods by raising an embankment, but there is no running away from an epidemic. Like other villagers, he is superstitious. He believes that if a crow caws, calamities follow; and when a jackal cries, it is a good time to go on a journey. The cooing of the cuckoo is ominous. If one sees a black cat, mangoes, or empty jars on the eve of a journey, some untoward event will occur. If a statement is followed by the "ta-ta" of a lizard, its truth is confirmed.

Religious functions are arranged in the village at different times of the year for religious education and also for raising subscriptions for the construction of a mosque or other sacred monuments. Meetings are also held by the *Tablighi Jamaat* (a missionary group) in the village. In addition to participation in all these activities, Suraj Mia also helps to settle disputes among the villagers. He also occasionally enjoys attending *Puthi* readings and story-telling assemblies. In this way, Suraj Mia reduces the misery of his insecure and difficult life.

Having presented a short description of the lives of two Muslim villagers, we shall now discuss the problems of two Hindu villagers, who are scarcely different from their Muslim counterparts. The problems of village life are such that they affect Hindus and Muslims alike. These problems are essentially human, and relate to the perils and hazards faced by poor people in all the developing countries of South and Southeast Asia.

*Jamini Kanta.* Jamini Kanta is well known in his village, where his family have lived for three generations. His father, Daraknath, who was a farmer and had a small weaving business, died twenty years ago. Jamini had one brother and one sister who lived with him until their death.

Jamini Kanta is now in his early sixties. He can vividly recall the days of his childhood, when the yield of the land was more than it is today. At that time people could have two crops a year, and lived much better than they do now. He recalls a famine in the country during the first decade of this century when even the tanks had dried up and people prayed for rain in the scorching heat of the sun.

He is the third son of his parents. His two older brothers died during the life of their father. His two younger brothers are alive. He became the head of his family in 1942 when his father died. He was married at the age of twenty-one. His wife comes from a neighboring village. Their only daughter died at birth, which he still recalls with emotion.

His attitude toward government policies of development is quite vague. He is not aware of any perceptible change or development in the village situation or that government officers have changed for the better.

Jamini Kanta is both superstitious and religious. He would not do anything without consulting the scriptures. He has visited the holy places of the Hindus, and performs all his religious obligations with punctuality. He celebrates *Durga Puja, Saraswati, Laxmi Puja,* and *Kali Puja* regularly. For recreation, *Jatra* and *Keertan* parties are arranged in the village. In April every year he goes to a *Mela* (fair) in a neighboring village.

Jamini has two acres of land with a yield sufficient for the needs of his small family. The yield, however, is always uncertain because of recurrent floods and cyclones. When these come he thinks it is the will of God, against which people have no power.

Jamini wants to spend the rest of his life in the old, traditional way. Although he himself never attended school, he believes that the younger generation should go to school and make the best of the social and economic changes coming to the country.

*Jagabandu Ghosh.*  Jagabandu, during his seventy-five years of life, has seen many ups and downs in his village. He finds the world changing too rapidly for him. He fondly recalls the picture of a happy Hindu family in this village about fifty years ago. His father had little education; but he had about fifteen acres of agricultural land, a considerable number of tenants, and a thriving money-lending business. His cattle shed was full of cows and bullocks, and his barn was never empty. But he sighs that, with the change of times, everything is changed and he has to face deprivation and want.

His father remarried after the death of his mother in a cholera epidemic. He had four brothers. From childhood he was unambitious and content with life in the village. Although his father tried to give him an education, he was not interested and quit school in the primary classes. At seventeen he married an illiterate girl he had not known before. She gave him two sons and five daughters.

His father died when Jagabandu was twenty-five years old. Being the oldest son, he became head of the family. At that time he had five unmarried brothers and sisters. Although the family size was expanding, he did not fail in his duty and looked after all of them.

Problems began to multiply with time. There were crop failures owing to drought and flood, and he had to mortgage land for the expenses of marriage and *Puja* festivals. In spite of all these calamities he tried to give his sons a proper education; but his sons, like himself, were not eager to go to school. His daughters were eager, but there were no facilities for female education in the village.

Jagabandu is a little more enlightened than the average villager. He explains economic hardship in terms of the increasing number of mouths to feed and the heavy expenses incurred on the occasions of marriage and *Puja* festivities.

These four villagers represent the bulk of the village population in East Pakistan. There is in all of them a general sense of insecurity and helplessness against the vagaries of nature and a consequent dependence and faith in religion, God, and the Unseen. The chapters that follow should be read with them in mind.

Thus we have presented background information about the people studied, as is the usual procedure in a sociological study. We shall now discuss the respondents themselves—their personal background, aspirations and frustrations, and general adjustment to village life in East Pakistan.

Like their parents before them, all our respondents, both Muslims and Hindus, have always lived in a village, and most of them in the villages under study.

In terms of their occupation also, both main and subsidiary, they are typical of the rural population. The majority of the village people in East Pakistan are cultivators with small landholdings. The subsidiary occupations include weaving, milk-selling, fishing, indigenous handicrafts, and casual labor. There may, however, always be a few persons in most villages who have gone to the nearby town in search of a job. But they would be an exception rather than the rule. In some villages there may also be a few professionals with special trades or skills, like the village medicine man (*Kabiraj*) or the teacher who may also act as the *imam* of the village mosque.

The choice of the subsidiary occupation for a villager would depend, in most cases, upon the location of the particular village, near or away from a town or a river. In a remote village, for example, the villager would either work on his own land or on someone else's land as a manual laborer at the time of sowing and harvesting. In a village near a town also there would be a majority of farmers, although they would have more frequent contact with the town either for selling their produce or for taking some odd job there. In a village near a river there would be a number of fishermen with little agricultural land.

Our two villages being near a district town have certain special features. Besides being farmers, a few of the villagers are in business, and more of them have subsidiary occupations as skilled or semiskilled laborers. Others visit the town to market their produce. All of them, however, are essentially rural in their attitudes and behavior.

The general village situation from the respondents' point of view has not changed during the last fifty years. Their perception of the various changes occurring in the country is one of the remote outsider. They feel that if things have changed or improved, the beneficiaries are not they but others living elsewhere. However, they observe the changes in the townspeople or in the younger generation of their own village. For them, though, the same toil and struggle remain. We found that 50 per cent see no difference in their situation since Independence, 40 per cent find themselves worse off, and only 10 per cent feel that their situation has improved. In general, therefore, the respondents have no cause for rejoicing in the recent changes because there is hardly any difference for them and, if at all, the balance is on the wrong side, owing to floods, cyclones, and the rising prices of consumer commodities. All of them feel that the frequency of natural calamities has increased during the last fifteen years.

When questioned about whether they would prefer to stay in their present occupation, mainly agriculture, or change, most of the respondents preferred to change, for both economic and social reasons. For example, government jobs have a stable and fixed income, which along with the "authority" attached to such jobs, would be prestigious in the eyes of the other villagers. Fourteen per cent of the Muslims and 51 per cent of the Hindus said they would prefer to enter some sort of business if given a chance. There was also a preference for government service, more among Hindus than among Muslims. But the main reason most respondents would want to go into an occupation other than agriculture is because of the economic insecurity of agriculture in East Pakistan today.

To reinforce our assumptions further we asked the respondents to specify those aspects of their main occupations that they liked and disliked most. Although their responses were not very clear, they did indicate the dominant economic reasons both for their positive and for their negative attitudes toward agriculture. The responses also indicated a certain conflict between the positive and the negative attitudes toward agriculture, and may be indicative of a value conflict between the peasant's love of land (Redfield, 1956) and the hard facts of life. While both Muslims and Hindus reported that they neither liked nor disliked agriculture, it may be said that the Hindu respondents liked it less.

It is my guess, however, that this ambivalence of the villagers toward agriculture as an occupation is of recent origin. Four or five decades ago the villagers' attitude toward agriculture may have been quite positive. Floods and cyclones were less frequent, the population pressure was less, and the yield from the land could last them till the next harvesting season. The amenities of life were cheaper and there were very few things within the individual's level of aspiration that were beyond him. The situation has changed drastically. The demands of existence have increased; the population is multiplying and landholdings are being divided and subdivided; and above all, nature is neither as kind nor as generous as before.

Understanding the attitudes of the villagers is, of course, basic to understanding the village culture. When the villagers were asked why they did not change from farming to another occupation, 72 per cent of the Muslims and 9 per cent of the Hindus replied, as would be expected, that they had no knowledge of any other kind of work.

We also asked the respondents to choose among the occupations of their friends and relatives, most of whom were also farmers and, therefore, no better or worse off than the respondents. The respondents did show an interest in the subsidiary occupations of their friends and relatives. Their choice of occupations were as teachers, businessmen, office workers, and medical practitioners. The occupation chosen most often was that of teacher, which, besides the pecuniary benefits involved, may be indicative of the respect villagers hold for an educated man. In general, however, their choices were determined by a quest for economic security and social prestige.

Based on the responses to our various questions, it would seem that cultivation of one's own land is no longer considered particularly respectable or rewarding, and is bereft of any psychological compensation. On the other hand, a job with a fixed income, however low, provides both economic and psychological rewards in terms of economic security and social prestige. This change in attitude is slow-moving, but quite significant, as was indicated when the respondents named persons in the village whom they respected. There was agreement on six men in the two villages. On inquiry it was found that these respected villagers were either educated or had a large landholding or, as in four cases, both. Two of them were doctors with a medical certificate, one was a cooperative organizer, and the other three had useful contacts in the town. Four of these six village "guides" had more than ten acres of land in addition to their income from subsidiary work. All were better educated than the rest of the village.

A similar attitudinal change is reflected in the frequent migration of the educated village youth to the towns and cities. Village life has so few comforts to offer that as soon as a boy gets enough education to qualify for a job in the town, he wishes to leave the village. There is no resistance to this idea on the part of the older villagers, who willingly and often enthusiastically encourage their sons to take up work and enjoy the amenities of urban life. This general desire for a better life does not always find expression overtly because of the prevailing fatalistic attitude to life on the part of the villagers. They are generally resigned to their lot, and may even shrug their shoulders if confronted with the idea of changing their occupation and residence in an effort to improve it. The reasons given by those who expressed a desire to change their way of life were (i) they wanted to live in society like human beings, (ii) they wanted to be able to educate their sons, (iii) they wanted more land and improvements in agriculture, and (iv) other jobs paid more money.

Further clarification of the desire for change indicates that while there is still a small group who do not believe any change in their life is possible, there is a larger group of villagers who do believe in the possibility of change, but not through their own efforts. The general attitude of both these groups is indicative of the same fatalistic attitude of helplessness and desperation. We have emphasized earlier that the villagers in East Pakistan have lost all faith in themselves, and look to the government for improvement of their lot. They believe that if the situation is to be changed, it can be changed only with help from others, help from the government, and help from God.

From these responses it is clearly indicated that the villager in East Pakistan is a frustrated individual. There are a number of reasons for this widespread dissatisfaction with village life. He has no steady income, and is unemployed most of the year. Crops are never adequate, so there is never enough to eat. Even a seemingly rich crop may be reduced to mere straw in a few hours (Schuler and Zaidi, 1961). There is no money for various household needs. Loans and debts keep multiplying, and there is no hope of their repayment. There are also family quarrels and village factions. Disease is widespread, and there is no money for the doctor and the medicine when the children fall ill. Nor are there educational facilities in the village. Thus there is a general sense of helplessness, brought on primarily by economic insecurity. And there is no hope, as the villager perceives, for any alleviation of his difficulties. Some villagers can look forward to their sons' growing up and bringing about an improvement in their economic situation. Others cannot.

There is a general impression among the urban educated classes in Pakistan that the villager is an essentially lazy man who whiles away his time either in useless gossip or in sleeping and procreating. This impression is not well-founded, and is unfair. Some respondents admitted spending their spare time in gossip, singing, sleeping, and praying; but one should not overlook the fact that for a villager in East Pakistan there are no other recreational facilities. Realizing the stresses of life in the village, one would be surprised if the villagers did not engage in some sort of relaxation. It is also a question of how one interprets spare time. Most of the villagers "look after their cattle, cut grass for the cattle or for selling it in the town" when they have spare time. Some of them even go to town and do rickshaw-pulling (tri-cycle) for extra money.

One of the customs of village life is for villagers to seek advice from a few people whose honesty and knowledge are greatly respected by the villagers. These are the village elders, who are usually consulted about family quarrels and other domestic problems. There is no consultation fee. Advice on religious matters and education is sought from the *imam* of the mosque and the *madrasah* teacher. Then there are the village touts, whom no one respects but to whom villagers go for advice because these men are believed to have influence with petty officials and knowledge of agricultural loans, court procedures, and revenue collections. One of the officials told me the story of a village tout who promised to help a villager by speaking to the subdivisional officer on his behalf when the officer came to inspect the village. The tout was paid some money in advance for "expenses" by the villager. When the officer visited the village, the tout told the man to stay at a distance and to observe him talking to the officer. The poor villager saw him with the officer and was satisfied that the tout had spoken on his behalf, while all that the tout did was to go to the officer, greet him with *"Salam-o-Alaikum,"* stay there for a few minutes, and go away. Most of the touts do nothing more than this, but are reimbursed for their "service."

It may be said, however, that some features of village life are undergoing change, especially in matters of communication between the village and the outside world. Villagers are being encouraged to seek advice from government officials, who, in turn, are instructed to be accessible to the villagers at all times.

# CHAPTER III

# THE VILLAGE FAMILY

AS IN OTHER PARTS of the world, the basic social unit in Pakistan is the family, which provides emotional, social, and financial security to its members. The resources of the entire family are pooled, and each man looks upon the head of the family as responsible for meeting all his needs and those of his wife and children. Each member is loyal to the family name, prestige, and property. Even when the individual units of the family are separated physically, the functional basis of all social activity is still the joint household.

The village family is generally an extended one in which sometimes two or three generations live together. Unlike the head of the family in an industrial society, the family head in the villages of East Pakistan is not necessarily the breadwinner. In almost all the villages in the Pak-Indian subcontinent, the oldest man in the family usually remains the head, and is consulted in important decisions about the children, property, and marriage. Often fifty-year-old sons obey their father as if they were still children.

When a number of brothers, along with their individual families, live in a joint household, there are occasional misunderstandings, mostly brought about by wives who do not like to live under the authority of the mother-in-law or the oldest brother's wife if the oldest brother is the head of the family. On such occasions the brothers must work out a settlement of the differences so that all may live peacefully. Occasionally, such petty quarrels result in division of the households and, perhaps, of the property. Even so, the brothers would still help each other as before should necessity arise.

Traditionally, the village family is the source of training for its children. Both male and female children remain the responsibility of the mother or the grandmother until they are ready to go to school or out to the field to work. The mother does not normally punish the child. She is most often protective and permissive. If a child misbehaves, the mother may threaten to tell his father. The role of the father is only peripheral in the early life of the child; but the image of the father created in the mind of the child is one of authority and power.

Because our contact for the present study was with the men in the village only, we tried to determine the relationship between the father and the children by first establishing the amount of time the father spends with his children. While we could arrive at no definite time interval, it seemed clear that the father in a village family is always available to his children, and that he cares for them by putting them to sleep, by playing with them, and, at times, by disciplining them. Through this type of association he helps his children to learn his trade, and instills in them the values and traditions of the family and the community.

The relationship between the child and the father always remains one of affection and respect. The father exercises authority over the entire family without consciously appearing to be authoritative, restrictive, or stern. If he feels the need, he chides the child or even beats him. In spite of this situation the relationship of affection and respect is never disturbed. The role of a father in the village is a harmonious balance between a strict teacher and a sympathetic and informal friend.

Since a majority of the respondents are almost illiterate, it may be instructive to know their way of teaching manners and discipline to their children. It appears from the interview records that the only method of teaching known to the villager is through punishment, which, of course, is not encouraged in modern educational practices. The villager, however, still believes in the old adage of "spare the rod and spoil the child." Yet in spite of this crude method of teaching, the village father is quite discriminating in his punishment. He does not punish the child for trivial misbehavior or for whiling away his time in innocent activities. The most frequent reason for which a child would be punished is disobedience in any form. This attitude reflects one of the very fundamental values of the society. Respect for the elders is a very important virtue in village society, and disregard of it is not tolerated by the family. In giving the reasons for punishing their children, the majority of the respondents said, "When they disobey me." The second reason given was, "If they do not read." Thus it would seem that the village father is particularly concerned about the behavior, moral and social conduct, and the future career of his children. He would not hesitate to beat them if this were the only method of correcting them.

In Pakistan society it is generally the parents who decide the future careers of their children, although this situation is now more prevalent in the villages than in the towns and big cities. The father, or the oldest member in the family, being the head, must constantly keep in mind the future of the children. We have, therefore, to visualize the hopes and fears of a village father in order to understand the dynamics of present-day rural society and the course the new generation is likely to follow.

In view of our general assumption regarding the attitude of the villagers to the agricultural calling, it was expected that most of the parents would wish their children to fare better in life than they themselves have done; that they would like their sons to become more prosperous, have a better education, and, if possible, obtain employment in a government service. The answers we received about the future hopes of the parents for their sons were that they be educated, that they be well behaved, that they be good farmers, that they have a sense of honor, and that they be good businessmen. As expected, the most frequent response (86 per cent) was in favor of the children's getting more education; for a good education means that they will not remain petty agriculturists, but may be able to get a government job and be like those officers who come to the village with an army of servants, peons and *chowkidar*s, and many other amenities and facilities—these accomplishments are what a poor farmer would expect of a well-educated son. What constitutes success now is quite different from what constituted success fifty years ago, when a village father wished his son to be a good farmer with a large property. This difference also supports the fact emphasized earlier that the rewards of an agricultural calling, under present village conditions, are so uncertain that even the traditional dislike for service is now pushed aside.

It is assumed that under the present village conditions a village father who desires his son to get an education and a good job would hardly want him to continue living in an unhealthy village, but would expect him to move to a city where he could have all the benefits of modern life. While the responses in this connection were not definitive, a good portion of both the Muslim and the Hindu respondents seemed to justify our general idea. There were only a few respondents who wanted their sons to continue to live in the village. The other two replies indicating indecision on the part of the respondents were, "Anywhere he likes to live," and, "I shall decide when the time comes." These responses indicate no definite desire on the part of the village father to have his son live in the village and, in his characteristically fatalistic attitude of resignation, he pretty much leaves it to the future. These responses also indicate the thinking of the present-day East Pakistan village farmer, who has no great desire to remain a farmer or to see his children do so if they can escape.

When questioned about those qualities deemed characteristic of a good son, most Muslim respondents said a good son would get a good education and a good job in order to care for his parents in their old age. Obedience and regularity in offering prayers were also mentioned. The Hindu respondents emphasized doing good works and getting a good education and a good job in order to enhance the prestige of the family. They also appreciated the quality of obedience to parents and other good habits. The differences in the attitudes of the two groups should be considered in terms of their recent sociopolitical experiences, which led to the partition of British India into the two independent Muslim and Hindu states, Pakistan and Bharat.

It may be worthwhile also to note what a village father expects from his daughter. In the context of the village culture the role and status of a daughter are different from those of a son. The son is expected to support and to look after the comfort of his parents in their old age. The status of the son in the family, therefore, is higher because of the expectation that he will be useful to the parents as long as they live, whereas the daughter leaves the parents after her marriage. A daughter in a traditional village family is not expected to provide financial support to the parents even if she could; parents would be ashamed to accept financial help from a daughter or her husband.

Those qualities deemed essential in a good daughter among Muslim fathers were that she perform her studies and religious obligations regularly. The Hindu fathers responding emphasized the importance of her doing good works, studying hard, conducting herself properly, and obeying her husband. The real difference in the attitude of the two groups of respondents is more a matter of emphasis than anything else. The generally accepted criteria, both for Hindus and for Muslims, for a good daughter in a village family are that she should be of good moral character, of irreproachable behavior, and be a good housekeeper for her husband's family. For Muslims, additional virtues for a daughter are strict observance of *pardah* (custom of a woman's being veiled in public) and regularity in prayers and fasting. For Hindus, the same virtues, put differently, are that she enhance the family name through her good reputation and virtuous life.

In contrast to the approved behavior of sons and daughters in the village, we asked both Muslim and Hindu fathers to indicate behavior among their children that would shame the family. Our respondents strongly asserted that the children in their village were well behaved and did nothing to shame their parents. Only about half of the Muslims responded to the question. Of those responding, inattention to studies and addiction to gambling (card-playing is considered gambling in the village) were considered shameful behavior. Keeping bad company and disobedience were also disliked. The Hindu parents (all of whom responded) placed the keeping of bad company and gambling as the most shameful behavior; but inattention to studies, disobedience, and misuse of money were also disapproved. The large difference in the response of the Muslims and the Hindus may be owing to the fact that Muslim fathers have high expectations from their children in a newly independent Muslim state. They may, therefore, tend to minimize the faults of their children. The Hindu respondents, on the other hand, may have no such expectations and are probably more objective.

In East Pakistan villages, marriage is an important occasion for everyone in the village. It is technically a social and legal contract between a couple, but owing to the religious orientation of the people, it has acquired a deep religious significance. The customs and ceremonies are clearly defined. There may be differences in the amount of money spent on individual marriages, but essentially the ceremonies are the same for the rich and the poor. There are, of course, differences between Muslim and Hindu marriage customs. While among Muslims marriage between cousins and other near relatives is permitted and sometimes preferred, among Hindus such a marriage is discouraged and often prohibited. Among Hindus, a marriage will not be arranged without a satisfactory dowry's being paid by the bride's family to the bridegroom. In theory, a Muslim marriage is a much simpler and less costly affair; however, because of their close contact with Hindus, Muslims frequently invoke the dowry system, especially in East Pakistan.

Under Muslim law, marriage is to be finalized only after the bride and the bridegroom have approved of each other at the *nikah* (acceptance) ceremony; but this ceremony is now only a formality, for in most cases the marriage has already been decided by the parents. Patriarchal authority prevails in marriage arrangements in the villages of both East and West Pakistan. Women are less free to choose than men. Owing to their lack of education and enlightenment, village women are, for the most part, ignorant of their legal rights and accept their subordination to men. They may even prefer this relationship in certain cases. And because village girls have no occasion to meet men, they would probably prefer that their parents choose for them, even if they were given a choice. In the cities, however, more and more frequently parents cannot arrange a marriage for their son without first asking his preference. The situation for girls in urbanized towns and cities is very little different from that of village girls, except in those families where the parents have become very westernized.

Generally, three ceremonies are performed in connection with marriage among Muslims. The first is the *nishan* ceremony, in which the guardians of the bridegroom go to the house of the bride with the gift of an ornament, some clothing and toilet articles for the bride, sweets, and betel leaves and nuts. Often even younger brothers, nephews, or cousins of the groom also accompany this party to the bride's house. This ritual may be taken to mean a sort of engagement, announced through the exchange of gifts.

A recent sociological study of Lahore district in West Pakistan reports similar rituals performed by Muslim villagers. At the time the father and the younger brothers meet the bride, who is decorously dressed for the occasion. The date of the wedding is set, and the terms of the transaction and the amount of the *mehr* (consideration for the contract of marriage) are also settled between the two respective guardians of the persons to be wed. All of these terms are written out in a formal document called the *fard* (account, or estimate). These procedures confirm the engagement of the couple.

The second ceremony is the marriage itself. Before the *barat* (bridal party) is ready to leave for the house of the bride, the groom is given a ceremonial bath. Usually the brother-in-law (sister's husband) is required to fetch water for the bath. The mouth of the pitcher is covered with decorated napkins or kerchiefs. The brother-in-law pours water on the groom. There is generally a mock fight for the possession of the napkins between the brother-in-law and the younger brothers and cousins of the groom. It develops into a hilarious party, with members throwing colored water or balls of soft soil on each other.

Both the bride and the groom in their respective houses apply an emulsion of *mehdi* leaves to the palms of their hands. This emulsion turns their palms a crimson color. The sisters-in-law make merry, dancing and singing around the bride and groom, and wishing them a happy and fruitful conjugal life.

The bridal party, comprised of the groom, his relatives, friends, and the important elders of the community, goes to the house of the bride. The party carries with it sweets, clothes, and ornaments for the bride. A gate is set up just in front of the house. When the bridal party reaches the gate, it is closed with bamboo barriers. The younger male and female relatives of the bride then ceremoniously block the bridegroom's way and insist that he pay them money or gifts to be allowed to enter through the gate. A bargain is then struck between the two parties, after which the bridal party is let in. When the members of the bridal party enter the marriage *pandal,* generally decorated with multicolored papers, they are served hot drinks.

The *nikah* is then performed with the mutual consent of the couples. The consent of the bride is obtained by a group of persons who become *vakil*s (witnesses) to her consent. The *maulvi* or the *qazi* (Muslim judge) then performs the religious part of the ceremony. The marriage register records the signature of the bridegroom, and the marriage is final.

A feast is then laid out. The groom, who is the chief guest of the party, is the first one to eat. The members of the bridal party return to the village with the bride. The bride, after staying for two days at the house of the bridegroom, returns to her house with her husband, accompanied by some younger brothers or cousins of the husband. This is the third and the last phase of the ceremony, called *phirani,* or the return visit. Another feast, known as *walima,* after the consummation of the marriage, is held at the house of the bridegroom before the departure of the bride for her home.

The actual marriage ceremony is uniform all over Pakistan and also among Muslims in India. The specific details of the rituals and rites, however, may vary from place to place.

With this general description of the marriage customs, we now return to our respondents. It was found that among Muslims the majority of the couples belonged to the same extended family. The premarriage relationship in most cases, therefore, was that of a cousin with brotherly or sisterly affection. The respondents indicated their preference for such marriages and, even if given a choice, would not have liked to marry outside the family. This preference indicates the strong familial attachment and the rigidity of the traditional practice in the villages. There are cases in which children are promised in marriage at birth. This promise traditionally becomes an engagement and is, therefore, binding, unless the child, after coming of age, refuses to uphold the promise of his parents. If not at birth, marriages in the village are generally decided much ahead of time, sometimes even ten or twelve years before the couple come of age, particularly in the case of close relatives.

Our survey showed that of those marriages occurring between relatives, 70 per cent were from farming families with a similar socioeconomic background. There is a strong suggestion that the custom of intermarriage is prevalent among Muslim communities. Modern genetics notwithstanding, Muslims encourage marriage between cousins because they believe that similarity of background guarantees stability of the marriage and the family and because of economic reasons. According to the Muslim law of inheritance, a son is entitled to two-thirds share of his father's property; a daughter, to one-third share. Thus girls marrying outside the family would take away their share of the property to their husband's family.

All the marriages in the two villages were arranged by members of the family—in most cases by the father or the oldest brother. There were also uncles, cousins, and brothers-in-law who took part in the marriage negotiations. The young couple were not consulted about each other's suitability. In a few cases, however, friends were commissioned by the elders to get the reaction of the bridegroom. But usually the negotiations are made, a dowry is agreed upon, and the date of the wedding ceremony is set before the couple hear about it, usually from their friends, who may have been coached by the parents to convey the news. This means of telling the couple may be a precaution of the parents before the final settlement so that if there is a negative reaction from the couple, and particularly from the man, they can take care of it in good time. However, in most cases the young man and woman are simply told that they are to be married to the daughter or son of such and such a person. The young couple, aware of the cultural demands and generally adhering to the community values and beliefs, accept these proposals without grumbling or resistance.

The respondents in our sample admitted that they had not seen their wives before marriage. It is, however, possible that they had known each other as children if they were from the same village or if they were close relatives living in neighboring villages. Since *pardah* is strictly observed among Muslims in East Pakistan, the Muslim respondents, even if they had known their wives before the wedding ceremony, would not have seen them after the age of puberty, at about twelve or thirteen. Thus Muslim marriages occur between two persons who may be familiar with each other's family background, but who have virtually never met before.

In the choice of a mate many factors are taken into account; namely, the cultural background of the family, age, religion, education, and the economic prospects of the bridegroom. The degree of emphasis on each of these factors differs from family to family. In recent times among the educated classes, the importance of individual and personal accomplishments has, however, increased. Till recently, marriage at all social levels was solemnized for the purpose of raising a family, but now in the urban sections of the population the concept of marriage has changed slightly from raising a family to looking for a companion in the other partner. The difference in the attitude to marriage between the rural and urban population is still, however, a matter of degree.

In this change of attitude many old and aristocratic families with great pride in their cultural background have lost their attraction for the marriageable young men and women because their sons and daughters have remained little educated, their only qualification being their family pride, which cannot measure up to the urban and industrial values of personal accomplishment.

Of course, the criteria for determining the qualities of a good wife vary among different cultures. In arranged marriages a wife is chosen for those qualities held important by the parents or elders arranging the marriage, whereas in a marriage resulting from courtship, those qualities held important by the bridegroom determine his choice. In the two villages under study, where the first course is followed, the majority of our Muslim respondents felt that the selection of their own wife was based on her skill at looking after the house, being a good cook, being able to sew, taking care of the cattle, and having a fair complexion. Other qualities mentioned by a few of the Muslim respondents were that she be regular in her prayers and fasting, of good moral character, of good family, educated, and that her dowry included some property. Among the Hindus, the majority made no response. Life for a good village wife is not easy. She must do everything inside the home and also look after her husband when he is working in the field. Only the skillful woman with a capacity to work hard can succeed as the wife of a village farmer under financial hardship.

In view of the poor economic condition of the villages, the most important aspect of a village marriage is the expense involved. The marriage ceremony has become a symbol of the family's social and financial status and of its conformity to the customs and traditions of the community. The higher the ascribed social status, the greater the tendency to show off on such occasions. It was therefore interesting to learn that the expense incurred in a typical marriage ceremony could be as much as *Rs.* 1,000 (about $200), although there were many of our respondents who recalled an expenditure of less than *Rs.* 500 in their marriage. Considering the importance attached to a marriage ceremony, one should expect that the villager would wish to spend even more, if possible. However, responses indicate that the majority of the village people do not like this heavy expense, and feel that it would be better if less money were spent for weddings.

Because this amount of money is more than a village family can easily afford, we assumed that most of the families had to borrow the money for a wedding, and were concerned with the social compulsion that made them go into debt for a ceremony that could easily have been avoided. We found that most village families did, indeed, have to borrow money to pay for the wedding of their sons and daughters. In almost all cases, the father or older brother borrowed the money. Unlike marriages in western countries where a young man is expected to be able to cover the expense of getting married, the village youth in East Pakistan, and generally throughout the Pak-Indian sub-continent, does not have to bother about the expense of his wedding. It is the concern of the parents and other relatives. Sometimes the entire joint family is involved. It may seem strange to the western observer that village families would borrow money for frivolous ceremonies, but such ceremonies are very important in the social life of a community not possessing external status symbols.

As mentioned before, because of the Hindu influence, even Muslim families are compelled to present dowries to the bridegroom, often well beyond their means. Although the custom is dying out among the Muslims, the bridegroom's family still expects the bride's father to give his son-in-law enough to establish a home. Such compensation is in the form of ornaments or money. In some cases the respondents said they got some very negligible items; but the majority said that, at the time of their marriage, they received money, clothes, utensils, a pair of bullocks, a ring, a wrist watch, some land, and ornaments. Many of these articles are needed to begin a household. The usual gifts of a father to his daughter are clothes, utensils, one or two ornaments, and some money.

It was found that in the majority of cases, the family of the bride was about equal economically and socially to the family of the groom. In a few cases, the bride's family was slightly better off financially than the groom's, but in no case was the situation reversed. This seems to be the general pattern among arranged marriages. The father of the groom always looks for a richer family from which to choose his daughter-in-law; and the father of the bride accepts this situation because there is a greater responsibility for a daughter than for a son, who is never a liability to a family.

Another aspect of marriage in a Muslim community is the number of wives a man may have at one time. Muslims are, by law and by custom, permitted to have as many as four wives at a time. However, the husband must be sure to treat all of them equally and justly. It is generally believed that in East Pakistan villages some men have more than one wife. Occasionally, they marry the widow of a brother as a second wife just to save her from economic insecurity. Often a number of wives are a great help in the field and, therefore, a great help economically. However, in our sample only one respondent had more than one wife. When we asked the respondents about their attitude towards taking another wife, they all said they would not; nor would they like for their sons to have more than one wife. Their reasons for this decision were that polygamy increases family quarrels, misery, and sorrow, and that it is not possible to provide for more than one wife under their present economic situation. A few of the Hindu respondents also said that they condemn the idea of more than one wife under any circumstances.

Divorce is a simple procedure under Islamic law. All that is required is that a man say, "I divorce you" three times in the presence of witnesses. Even so, divorce is a very uncommon phenomenon in Pakistan society. It occurs more often in urban areas than in rural, and more often between couples whose marriage was not arranged.

It is generally assumed that rural people are more religious minded than urban people and that they observe the customs and rules of the community more strictly. Muslims everywhere in the Pak-Indian subcontinent generally believe in keeping a woman confined to the four walls of the house. When going out, she must observe *pardah*, by concealing her face with a long, loose, robelike covering known as a *burga*, which is wrapped over the usual dress and serves to hide her from the supposedly evil and capricious eyes of strangers. One of the basic values of Muslim communities is that a woman, be it the wife, mother, sister, or daughter, has duties inside the home. She is expected to look after the children and the men in the family, provide them with all comforts, cook the food, and look after the general cleanliness of the house. This is one of the important rural behavior patterns for women. In the cities, however, we do not find any very strict adherence to this pattern.

Muslims in East Pakistan villages are particularly religious minded. We find more persons going to the mosque for daily prayers than in other parts of the country. A larger number of men fast during the holy month of Ramadan (one of the pillars of the Islamic faith) in East Pakistan. It was assumed, therefore, that most Muslim women in the villages would observe *pardah*, and data indicated that 98 per cent of them do. A stranger in the village would hardly see a girl above ten years of age. The observance of *pardah* begins at about the age of twelve; but in many cases it may be even earlier because the age concept of the villager is not very reliable.

Since the original concept of *pardah* has been distorted in practice everywhere, each family has made its own list of persons in whose presence the women are to be veiled. Most families in our study require that *pardah* be observed in the presence of strangers and the elders of the family—those who are termed *na-mahram*—particularly for young wives.

We were also interested in the attitude of the villagers toward *pardah* because, in certain cases, one may prescribe it for the women in the family and still not believe in its usefulness. The responses indicated that almost everyone believes in the usefulness of the *pardah* system as such, and prefers that his wife, sisters, and daughters observe strict *pardah* against strangers and distant relatives. The women also seem to accept is as a necessity. In spite of a number of urban values invading the mores of the present-day rural communities, *pardah* still remains very much as it was thirty or forty years ago, and is considered one of the essential virtues of a good Muslim woman.

Among the Hindus in East Pakistan villages, *pardah* is not observed as strictly. Since most of the Hindus in our sample belong to the lower caste, *pardah*, as an accepted virtue of the female population, is not prevalent among them. Among the high-caste Hindus in India, *pardah* was strictly observed about twenty years ago. *Pardah* is thus not altogether unknown to the Hindu community. Lower-caste Hindus even elsewhere in India are not very particular about *pardah.*

*Pardah* has come to have religious significance for Muslim families, and most of the East Pakistan villagers look upon it as such. It is a general stereotype of the villager that a non-*pardah*-observing woman does not have a good moral character. This stereotype guides the villager in his evaluation of any woman from outside the village. This judgment may also be related to some of the basic social norms of the village. For example, a city women without *pardah* may be treated just like a man, and may not be allowed to enter freely the living quarters of the village women. By the same token a career woman, a college woman, or a woman teacher does not fit into the social and moral picture of the villagers in East Pakistan.

The times of birth, circumcision, and death are observed with ceremony and ritual throughout Muslim Pakistan, as described below, with occasional variations (Slocum, Akhtar, and Sahi, 1959).

## Birth

Birth is always an occasion for rejoicing in villages where people are generally unconcerned with population pressures and the need for family planning. In families where there are not many children, parents even pray for the birth of a child. In general, the birth of a male child is preferred, hence the greater rejoicing on the birth of a baby boy.

A ceremony known in some parts of East Pakistan as *Panch Pitha* (five cakes) takes place during the fifth month of the pregnancy. On a particular day five kinds of cakes are prepared. Village women go to the house of the expectant mother and sing folk songs appropriate to the occasion. The mother-to-be wears a new dress. After the songs, the cakes are distributed to all.

The birth of the baby is also followed by distribution of sweets to friends and relatives who come to congratulate the parents. Some prosperous families give money and clothes to the poor in celebration. The parents soon choose a name for the baby. Close relatives, and in some cases the *maulvi,* suggest names. In many cases the naming ceremony is the occasion for a feast known as *Aqiqua*. There is a superstition in certain parts of East Pakistan against the mother's tasting the meat at this feast.

## Circumcision

Circumcision of sons is another occasion for Muslim families to renew kinship ties and enjoy a feast. In the villages, circumcision is performed mostly by the *hajjam* (barber), and the tool used for the purpose is a razor, knife, or any other sharp, metal instrument. This is also an occasion when friends and relatives present gifts to the boy.

## Death

The mouth and toes of the dead are tied up with a piece of cloth, the eyes are closed, the hands are straightened or folded over the stomach, and the face is turned towards the west, indicating the intention to face towards Kaaba, the Muslim holy place in Mecca. Relatives and friends come to see the dead person for the last time.

A new, long cloth for the coffin; camphor; and rose water are brought for the dead. Flowers are also brought, if possible. A thoroughly cleansing bath with hot water is given to the dead body. The body of a man is then wrapped up in three pieces of cloth; that of a woman, in five pieces; and that of an infant, in one piece. The body is laid on a bed, and camphor and rose water are sprinkled on it. Relatives and friends have a last look, and then the coffin is tied on both ends. The bed is carried on four male shoulders to the graveyard. A last prayer (*Namaz-e-Janaza*) is said in unison at the grave, and after the prayer, the body is lowered into the grave. The procession then returns to the house of the deceased.

For the first day or two after the death, no cooking is done in the house of the deceased, and meals for the survivors are sent from the homes of relatives and friends.

Three prayers are generally held for the deceased: the first one on the third day, the second on the seventh or ninth day, and the third on the fortieth day following the death.

The Hindus burn their dead near a river. Their ceremonies follow Hindu religious instructions.

These are the various aspects of the village family in East Pakistan. In many ways these aspects are similar to those in other parts of the Pak-Indian subcontinent. Owing to many recent social and technological changes, however, there are visible signs that the joint family as a rural social institution is passing through a difficult crisis presented by new and often contrasting values and attitudes.

# CHAPTER IV

# SOCIAL STRUCTURE AND CLASSIFICATIONS

IN A GENERAL SENSE the villages have both a formal and an informal social organization. Before the introduction of the Basic Democracies in 1960 there used to be a Union Board constituted with six to eight villages. The Union Board had a chairman and a few members. This group represented the formal leadership of these villages. This formal organization of the villages was quite powerful because of its official contacts with the government officers and, therefore, effected a liaison between the organization and its government counterpart—the circle officer. The villagers accepted the official authority of the Union Board members and especially that of the chairman, who, in turn, had to satisfy prominent villagers so that he would have their support in elections.

Since the introduction of Basic Democracies, the union boards have been replaced by union councils, and the office of the chairman is no longer elective through adult franchise. A number of nominated members have been added to the union councils. These changes have introduced in this formal organization of local self-government more official control and less community representation and authority, thereby weakening the authority of the Union Council chairman and members. This formal organization, the Union Council, is doing its best through development work for the villages, to regain its lost prestige and leadership. While it may succeed in its efforts to some degree, it will probably never replace the informal power structure that obtains in the villages at present.

The informal social organization of the village, as has

been pointed out earlier, is only loosely structured. But in spite of the looseness of its structure, it functions quite effectively in village affairs. This functional authority, though not apparent, is quite real. Its decisions, because of its traditional prestige, are often accorded more acceptance than those of the Union Council. This situation may be indicative of the villagers' attitude to official control in their affairs.

Arensberg and Niehoff (1964), while discussing the human social institutions, state that there are at least three major institutions through which men everywhere organize their social relationships, though there are varying degrees of emphasis on the different sections of these three institutions in accordance with the level of technological advancement of a given culture. These three institutions are based on the principles of (i) kinship, (ii) common geographical boundaries, and (iii) special interest groups. Our discussion of the East Pakistan village social organization will be in terms of these three bases of social relationships.

First, the principle of kinship. Kinship is the general basis of social organization in almost all developing societies. On the contrary, the more developed societies have the weakest kinship relationship. Like all developing societies with dominant agricultural orientation, East Pakistan villages also have strong kinship affiliations as the primary basis of sociocultural relationships. Kinship groupings, both in terms of spatial proximity and in terms of emotional closeness, bind closely related families (*kunba*) in the village into an integrated primary group who stand together through thick and thin. They help each other in quarrels and disputes with other village families or with outsiders. They are the first in all ceremonies and important occasions. They are often on the same side of a village faction. The larger the *kunba*, the stronger its leader, generally the oldest member, in the village power structure. An outsider can enter the *kunba* only through marriage. Each member of the group is very much aware of his and the *kunba*'s joint responsibilities toward relatives. This pattern of rights and responsibilities and the significance of each member of the kin is a strong force in the rural culture of East Pakistan.

The second basis of social organization for the village is the contiguity in the location of a number of families within a geographical boundary. It is a community of people who have been living together for many generations. Contiguous living within the geographical location has given rise to different social relationships among the villagers.

In each village there are certain families with landed property and other poorer families with little or no land. These poorer families depend for their subsistence on casual labor on the land of other families, or on more permanent jobs in or outside the village. These two classes of people in the village depend upon each other's help. There exists the relationship of the employer and the employee and the rich and the poor. In both capacities these families have a permanent relationship of mutual trust and dependence in times of need. The poor families get help from their more prosperous neighbors in time of need; the richer families employ the services of the poor people or even borrow their services for their festive or sad occasions. Thus this interdependent relationship may be conceived of as one type of social relationship, which though loose, is nonetheless quite functional. This system has some resemblance to the Hindu *jajmani* system, about which so much has been written (Wiser, 1936; Opler and Singh, 1948).

The other pattern of social relationship is that between the less informed and the more informed villagers. In most of the villages there are people who have contacts with the town and the outside world. The school teacher is better informed than the ordinary village farmer, and there is also the *imam* of the village mosque. These people have traditionally been the sources of information for the village, and by virtue of their better information and social contacts have wielded a certain influence in the village. They are a distinct social class.

In recent years with the increased number of education facilities, many young men have gone off to college and the university. If after their education they decide to settle in the village, they constitute a strong, influential force, especially in regard to agricultural and educational problems. As a matter of fact, they are taking over the leadership from the *imam*, the tout, and the *maulvi*s. Still an incipient social group in the villages of East Pakistan, in time they may become a force both formally and informally.

The last classification of village society that is fairly traditional and quite old is the division of the community into elders and elites on the one hand, and the rest of the villagers on the other. There is an informal village council in every village composed of the heads of the prominent families. There are generally the village *sirdar* and a number of *maatbar*s in the village council. The office of a *sirdar* is generally hereditary, and goes to the oldest son in the family. The office of the *maatbar* is also hereditary, but a new one can always be added. The *sirdar*s and the *maatbar*s can also be ousted if the villagers find that they lack the power of decision, or if they are found guilty of favoritism and dishonesty. Since the office is informal, the only indication of their ouster would be the fact that the villagers would stop consulting them.

The functions of a village *sirdar* are many and varied. He is the political and social advisor of the village. He is the civil and criminal court for village disputes. He is the liaison between the villagers and outside visitors and guests. All information about the village is available only through him if he is a strong and popular *sirdar*. In response to the confidence of the villagers, the *sirdar* must be the custodian of village morals and conduct. He must pay strict observance to the social and cultural norms of the community. He is generally one of the richest men of the village, and is expected to help people in time of need. The village council, over which the *sirdar* presides, is generally the supreme decision-making body in the village. All matters concerning the village are brought before this council. Customarily, the Union Council consults the *sirdar*s and *maatbar*s in matters concerning their village, if they are not already members of the Union Council, for the Union Council finds it difficult to impose a decision on a village against the village council, in whom usually the villagers have greater confidence than they have in the Union Council.

The informal village council, therefore, is a powerful body in the village social structure, although the recent increase

in the number of village factions has caused the disintegration
or at least a weakening of the village council. In such villages,
these special-interest groups have taken the place of the village
council. In the heyday of the village council, the *maatbar*s and
the *sirdar*s felt responsible for the welfare of the village, with
many of them even sacrificing their own private gains for the
benefit of the village, and thus earning the respect of the
villagers. They used to be inducted into "office" with great
ceremony. The following description, communicated to me
by a circle officer, relates the details of how *maatbar*s were
accepted as such by the villagers. It also explains the process
of decision-making by the informal leaders:

If a person wants to become a Maatbar the first thing he does
is to invite the other Maatbars and Sirdars of the surrounding
villages and entertain them. They would then acknowledge him
as a Maatbar. This ceremony over, the man will then be recognized
as a Maatbar in his village and in the surrounding villages.

If any dispute in the village is not settled by the Maatbars of
the village, the Maatbars of the surrounding villages will be invited
by the disputing parties and after thoroughly examining witnesses,
they will reach a decision about the dispute. The decision thus
reached is morally binding on the parties. Sometimes decisions
are thrust on the parties and if they do not accept the verdict
and the conditions of the decision, the villagers may resort to
their only means of social control, namely, a social boycott of the
person not obeying the decision of the Maatbars.

It may be noted, however, that rich people get away
with violations more easily than the poor, although this situation
may weaken the village informal body. With the increasing
number of young educated men in the villages, the pattern of
authority and the social organization are facing a great challenge, besides having engendered a deep conflict between the
traditional, old, and generally uneducated leadership and the
new, young, and educated enthusiasts who professedly are out
to improve the village through the use of their skill and knowledge.

To illustrate the pattern of social organization a specific
case from one of the villages under study is given below:

In terms of kinship this village has three families known after their original professional titles, *Qazi bari*, *Munshi bari*, and *Majumdar bari*. These three families represent the aristocracy of the village, and are accepted as the custodians of culture and refinement in the village. Each family has a *sirdar*, who is at present the head of the family. These families separately represent three different kinship groups in the village. They would always act in the interest of the family. The other village families are not so well knit and, therefore, cannot be called kinship groups. They represent themselves separately, and affiliate themselves with one or the other groups as the occasion demands.

At the village level, these *sirdars* of the three families are prominent. But there are a number of *maatbars* in the village also. The authority of the *sirdars* is weakened because of factions, which, at the moment, divide the village. The three *sirdars* are Amir, Ali, and Haque, but the other prominent persons in the village are the following:

*Rahim.* About forty-five years old, with a little education. He has eight *kanis* of land (the average landholding in this village is about four *kanis* per family). He also has a number of cattle, and sells milk. He is a former member of the Union Council.

*Suraj.* About thirty-eight years old, is a matriculate, and is locally qualified to practice medicine, from which he earns about one hundred rupees a month. He has twenty-six *kanis* of land, and is a member of the Union Council. His profession has brought him closer to the village people.

*Dutta.* About fifty-five years of age, and has the same medical certificate as Suraj, but his income from medical practice is about three hundred rupees a month. He has only four *kanis* of land, and is also a member of the Union Council. He is financially quite solvent, and this solvency has helped him in his leadership role.

*Nathu.* About fifty years old, read up to matriculation. He is a cloth merchant. He is also sound financially, in spite of having no land. He is intelligent, and quite active in village politics.

*Ali.* About fifty years old, and no education. He has

five *kani*s of land. His son's being a truck driver in the army has helped him socially in the village. He is also one of the *sirdar*s.

Three of these leaders are educated, and there are other young men in the village who have had some education. About one dozen people have had schooling up to the matriculation standard. There are a few persons in service in the town. There is one overseer in the construction and building department, one police constable, one manager of a small ice cream factory, one clerk in a tea company, and three primary school teachers. These people serve as the liaison between the village and the town, and serve as the villagers' channel of communication with the outside world.

At present the village is divided into two groups owing to some differences on the location of the village market. The traditional village social organization is powerless to prevent this division of the village primarily because other and more educated, stronger, and financially solvent leaders have replaced the traditional *sirdar*s, who have now become almost nonentities. Each of the faction leaders, while potentially capable of becoming the village leader, may not be acceptable to the villagers because they do not have the traditions of family leadership on their side. It may be another reason why they would like the faction to continue, because otherwise they may lose their leadership position in village affairs.

Social classes have always existed in every society, including the Muslim society, which has never been without them at any time in history. As a matter of fact there is no evidence of a classless society anywhere in the world. What differentiates one group from another is, therefore, not the existence or absence of social classes, but the bases on which various sections in the group are classified. In view of this fact, I was interested in finding out the bases for classifying different village families in East Pakistan which are Muslim in faith and character, but rural in their attitudes and behavior.

I initiated the inquiry with a general question about whether the village people make distinctions of high and low families and, if so, what the distinctions are. This question was followed by a long list of assumed bases of discrimination to be checked by the respondents. In response to the first question, all the Muslim respondents agreed that there are high and low families in the village. They further said that the distinction between families was made on the basis of landed property and other wealth. Seven per cent of them also mentioned education of the family members as a basis for social classification which, of course indirectly, could help to make the family wealthy through the ability of its members to hold a good job. It is, however, surprising that they did not mention family aristocracy as one of the bases of social classification. As a crude attempt to explain this omission, it can be said that the possession of landed property probably implies the family aristocracy that goes with the possession of land for many generations. Thus it seems that among the Muslim villagers today, wealth is the primary factor that places a family higher in the social hierarchy.

The responses of the Hindu villagers were varied, but quite in line with my expectations. It may be mentioned that the Hindu sample in this study belongs only to one professional class, viz. weavers; and, therefore, it is quite likely that there is no difference in their caste, since they all belong to the same level in the Hindu caste hierarchy. Forty-seven per cent of these respondents said that they do not regard any families as higher or lower, which means that they are all of the same social class. Thirty-five per cent of the Hindu respondents mentioned social status as the basis of classification. Social status is an ambiguous term in this context. On further probing it was found that they mean family status in the sense of Hindu caste hierarchy. Landed property was given as a basis by only 11 per cent, and money by only 22 per cent of the respondents.

It seems evident, therefore, that for Muslim respondents money and landed property are the bases of social distinction while for the Hindus it is family status, within the framework of the caste system. With this background information, I proceeded to find out the specific factors which place a village family socially higher or lower in the villagers' estimation. There were fourteen items of distinction, out of which some

## TABLE 10
Factors Determining Social Classification of Village Families

| Social Class Determinants | Per Cent of Muslims | | | Per Cent of Hindus | | |
|---|---|---|---|---|---|---|
| | *Yes* | *No* | *Do not know* | *Yes* | *No* | *Do not know* |
| Education | 100 | 0 | 0 | 87 | 0 | 13 |
| Wealth | 98 | 2 | 0 | 96 | 0 | 4 |
| Landed property | 97 | 2 | 1 | 96 | 0 | 4 |
| Age | 10 | 83 | 7 | 11 | 31 | 58 |
| Religious devotion | 18 | 72 | 10 | 93 | 0 | 7 |
| Color of skin | 3 | 91 | 6 | 0 | 31 | 69 |
| Number of men in the family | 46 | 51 | 5 | 11 | 27 | 62 |
| Government service | 95 | 3 | 2 | 78 | 11 | 11 |
| Brick house | 74 | 10 | 16 | 78 | 11 | 11 |
| Knowledge of the religious language | 72 | 9 | 19 | 96 | 0 | 4 |
| Number of houses | 72 | 12 | 16 | 0 | 34 | 66 |
| Number of children | 57 | 23 | 20 | 4 | 34 | 62 |
| Family descent | 79 | 12 | 9 | 85 | 2 | 13 |
| Holding of public office | 84 | 7 | 9 | 38 | 4 | 58 |

items generally considered unimportant were included to test the respondents' discrimination. It appears from the data given in Table 10 that all the villagers agreed on at least two items as being unimportant, namely, age and the color of the skin; and, therefore, these two items can be taken as unimportant even from their point of view. For the Hindus three other items—the number of houses, men, and children—were also unimportant for social classification. However, it may also be that the items not considered important by Muslim respondents were after all not so unimportant.

One can find a clear division between Hindus and Muslims especially in terms of the importance of certain items. This division may be owing to the differential perception of the items by the respondents in the context of their present sociocultural situation. It may also be owing to a basic difference of attitude and approach which is culturally conditioned. Another reason for the difference may be the significance of the present political situation for each of the two groups. To explain this point further, it may be noted that before Independence, in spite of the numerical majority of Muslims in this part of the country, Hindus enjoyed financial, social, and educational superiority, which, therefore, made them more self-confident than their Muslim neighbors. After Independence, however, the situation has changed drastically in favor of Muslims in East Pakistan. This change has caused a serious psychological blow to the Hindus, who are now a defeated group who have lost all enthusiasm and ambition for the political, social, and cultural life of East Pakistan.

The Hindus, with their attitude of defeatism, feel that they can no longer compete with Muslims for opportunities in education, government services, and public office. This fact is indicated from the differences in the frequency of responses to these items. Both the Hindus and Muslims assign high place to education and government service, but the Hindus are fairly lower than Muslims in terms of the frequency of their responses to these items. As to the importance of holding public office as a factor in social prestige, the frequency of Hindu responses is quite low (38 per cent), which may be indicative of their attitude toward holding public office in Pakistan.

However, there seems to be a general agreement among the Muslim and Hindu respondents that education, wealth, landed property, and family descent are the important factors that place a person or a family at a higher level than other villagers. Education, as one of the factors enhancing social prestige, is possibly the most recent addition to the villagers' perceptual field; and may be indicative of the social change that is coming to the villages. While wealth, landed property, and family descent have always been considered important in the rural social structure, an educated man was, in the past, respected for his attainments, but his education as against other traditional criteria hardly mattered in terms of raising his social prestige. Modern education now benefits the family in many ways, including respectable government jobs, contact with officers, and even comfortable urban living. Education in this sense is, however, still only the pious wish of most of the village families, which is why, in response to the previous question about the bases of social classification for the present village families, education as a factor did not receive much mention.

Besides these factors, government service, the possession of a *pucca* (brick) house, and the knowledge of the religious language (Arabic for Muslims, Sanskrit for Hindus) are also considered important for social prestige by the respondents. Government service and education seem to appear more important to Muslims. Only 78 per cent of the Hindu respondents mentioned these two factors, while 100 per cent of the Muslims mentioned education, and 95 per cent mentioned government service as important factors in social classification. A *pucca* house is a sign of present wealth, as well as an indication, in most cases, of the long aristocratic and wealthy background of the owner. Seventy-four per cent of the Muslims and 78 per cent of the Hindus mentioned this factor. Knowledge of the religious language may generally indicate the religious attainments of the person, but to a Muslim this may not necessarily be so. For Hindus, however, a person with a knowledge of Sanskrit can only be a Brahmin and, therefore, automatically quite high in the Hindu caste hierarchy. Ninety-six per cent of the Hindus, therefore, considered this an important factor. Among the Muslim respondents, only 72 per cent mentioned this item because, to them, social prestige is not the automatic result of a person's knowing the Arabic language. He must also be a good practising Muslim. The same attitude applies to the item regarding religious devotion, which 93 per cent of the Hindus and only 18 per cent of the Muslims mentioned as important. In Hinduism, religious devotion seems to be the monopoly of the priestly class, who are higher in the caste hierarchy and, therefore, higher socially. For Muslims, on the other hand, religious devotion is the duty of every Muslim man and woman, the benefits from which would come to the individual only in the life hereafter; hence devotion, as such, would not guarantee social prestige.

Age and color of skin were included in the list of items to see if the villagers could discriminate between relevant and irrelevant items. They did, which is indicated by the small frequency of their mention both by the Muslim and by the Hindu respondents.

Three items—the number of children, men, and *basha* (thatched hamlets)—were included as giving social significance to village families. The assumption was that the number of *basha*s possessed by a family may indicate property; the number of men, the fighting as well as the earning potential; and the number of children, the future wealth of the family. The response frequency of Muslims was 46 per cent, 72 per cent, and 57 per cent for the number of men, *basha*s, and children, respectively. The Hindus, however, do not seem to consider these items as being of any social significance, as indicated by the infrequency of their being mentioned. This indifference of the Hindus towards the number of men and children can possibly be explained in terms of the fact that most of the men emigrated to India after Independence; and the children, when grown, may do the same. This situation may be responsible for the Hindu indifference to the numerical strength of the family. Allied to this attitude is the fact that a family needs more *basha*s only when there are more men. Since Hindus do not attach much significance to numerical strength for a family's social prestige, they possibly consider it equally unimportant to possess a number of vacant *basha*s.

In summation, the general picture of the social classificaiton in East Pakistan villages that we get from the above analysis of responses appears to place education, money, and landed property as the three most significant bases. A village family can acquire status only if it has one or all of these three elements in its favor. The majority of village leadership comes from families with these qualifications. Education, of course, is something that has apparently been added recently, possibly because it is considered a useful means for the acquisition of money and landed property. An acceptance among villagers of education for its own sake is still a far cry away. Education, in our present society, is identified with a diploma or a degree, and very little with knowledge because one gets a good job if he holds a good degree, whatever his knowledge. This attitude toward education is not peculiar to villages. Urban centers also identify education with material comforts, social position, and an avenue of respect.

# CHAPTER V

# FACTIONALISM IN THE VILLAGES

THOUGH SOCIAL SCIENTISTS have recognized the significance of factions in the life of communities, no real systematic work has been done to understand the basis, organization, and membership motivations in factions. The few attempts made to describe factions constitute efforts to fit whatever data are available into a preplanned theoretical framework (Lewis, 1953). To understand a phenomenon like that of village factions in different cultural groups it is imperative, I think, to study its various dimensions without first building up a theory. Our knowledge about factions, in spite of Linton's suggestion over thirty years ago (Linton, 1936), still remains largely perfunctory, and the field unexplored.

The purpose of describing factions in East Pakistan in this chapter is not to support a theory but to emphasize with Lewis that factions take us to the very heart of village life. In the general framework of the present study, the purpose is to understand the East Pakistan village society. I shall discuss certain representative case studies of factions in our villages. In describing these cases, the primary purpose is to highlight some of the basic problems of village life, which could not be focused any other way. These problems are, in brief, of human interaction in the villages of today. I shall not be so much concerned with the faction membership and the resolution of the conflict as with the motives and the dynamic relationship of events leading to disruption and disunity in the otherwise peaceful life of the villages. But before going on to discuss the factionalism in East Pakistan villages, it may be useful to point out the similarities and differences of the only study available with which a meaningful comparison may be justified. This is Lewis' study of factions in an Indian village near Delhi.

Lewis conducted his studies in a Hindu Jat village near Delhi. The study of factions grew out of his interest in identifying village leaders. There were twelve castes in a population of 1,095. He noted twelve faction groups in this village. These factions centered around caste groupings, and the family was the basis of the faction structure. Thus he assumed these factions to be primarily kinship units, organized along caste lines. In his explanation regarding the reasons for these factions, Lewis noted that the fundamental cause was the insecurity of village life, and the specific causes related generally to money, women, and land.

No definition of the term faction was given by Lewis; neither was there an indication of how the term was used in related literature. It is difficult, therefore, to evaluate the thesis and conclusions of his study. As Pocock (1957) points out, the evidence offered by Lewis conflicts in several places with the conclusions drawn from it, and is also inadequate. Lewis' emphasis that factions are primarily a kinship unit, makes one feel that he probably confused close and cohesive family groups with factions. It is quite likely that the twelve subgroups, which he called factions, may have had close family constellations distinct from each other in terms of their more cohesive and closer interactions in relation to the entire community. Normally, factions, as I know them, do not exceed two or three in a village community. His counting of twelve subgroups as twelve factions, therefore, is most surprising. These subgroups may be caste subgroups that were bound by blood ties and came together on specific occasions for joint actions, not necessarily against another group. This point is clear from his statement about neutral and friendly factions. Factions, by definition, cannot be neutral or friendly. To a foreigner unfamiliar with the close family ties of the East and the sense of oneness and belonging, this conclusion may not be unusual. His second statement about factions being permanent and enduring may also be based on the same confused reasoning.

He traces the origin of factions in Rampur as far back as the last century. Factions normally do not last that long because there would be many intervening events to change both the composition and the motivations of a factional group.

In my studies of East Pakistan villages, there is some evidence that factions follow the kinship line, but not exclusively. As Firth (1957) points out, factions may rest upon kinship ties, patron-client relations, religious or politico-economic ties, or any combination of these groups. He also mentions a feature of factions in evidence in East Pakistan. Factions are loosely structured; tend to become activated on specific occasions; and operate, for the most part, in terms of total allegiance or commitment to the group and its position so that the issue is judged not on its own merits but in relation to a total strategy of opposition and alliance.

I do agree with Lewis that in East Pakistan also money, land, and women may be responsible for most of the factions resulting in overt conflict. But these three basic motives for human conflict are universal. In addition, many of the factions, as Lewis noted, are known by the name of their leaders, although in my study I found that the leadership itself is not enduring in many cases. There may be compromises in two factional groups against a third one, in which case one of the leaders will become secondary. Such cases are not rare in village factions.

Another study conducted only about fifty miles from Rampur and with a similar group of Jats has been reported by Inayatullah (1958). It was made in a village near the Lower Chenab Canal in West Pakistan, where also the majority of the landowning class were Jats and Tarars, another subcaste of the Jats. These were, however, Muslims. Though there is no caste among Muslims, in this particular village something similar to a Hindu caste is quite significantly present. For the villagers, caste and *patti* are significant social divisions in the village. Discussing factions, Inayatullah states:

It is a secondary group, superimposed on the other primary groups, sometimes running parallel, sometimes across them, seeking cohesion in order to ascertain power or to meet a similar challenge from another group ... its membership is more or less optional and not automatic like that of the family, caste or patti, it sometimes breaks these groups ... social inequality which is quite sharp otherwise, is reduced within the faction, as it is less determined by birth, or caste privileges and more by devotion to the cause of the group.

In this study, as should be apparent, faction loyalties go beyond the caste and *patti,* and are not based primarily on kinship ties. This situation is similar to those obtaining in East Pakistan in relation to faction composition.

There are other differences also between my faction cases and that of Lewis, primarily owing to the differences in the social organization of Hindu and Muslim villages. The most fundamental difference, I think, seems to be that in Lewis' Rampur, the factions center around different castes (Jats, Brahmins, etc.), whereas in a Muslim village, caste is replaced by social classification in terms of wealth and landed property; and, hence, is a less rigid determinant of community division into factions.

A second variation seems to be owing to the complication of the Hindu inheritance laws regarding adopted sons. Since among Muslims in East Pakistan adoption is almost unknown, I did not come across any factions of this nature.

Thirdly, there is no significance attached to the political causes of factions in Lewis' study. In East Pakistan, however, a majority of factions in the last analysis have political grievances; and since political issues necessarily involve the personalities of the contestants, factions in many cases revolve around the leaders of the two subgroups.

A fourth cause of the differential pattern of factions between Hindu and Muslim villages may lie in the fact of the relative ease of Muslim marriage and divorce procedures. Many of the factions in East Pakistan relate to divorce and marriage. Marriages between cousins and other relatives are quite common among Muslims, and, therefore, most of the time the villagers are involved on one or the other side of the marrying or the divorcing party. In a Hindu village such a situation will hardly occur. On the contrary, as Lewis points out, there are more intervillage than intravillage factional groups. Undoubtedly, caste and kinship among Hindus have their range beyond and across village boundaries. This was perhaps at the back of Lewis' statement about the Hindu village's not being a sociological reality (Lewis, 1954). The Muslim village on the other hand has more intravillage loyalties, and, therefore, is a sociological reality.

Besides, one cannot find much evidence for Lewis' statement that factions are caused mainly by the insecurity of village life, except as the maladies and troubles of the villagers can generally be attributed to their insecure position. There is, however, evidence to the contrary that, under times of stress from the natural calamities of floods, cyclones, or droughts, factions tend to dissolve and the villagers come to each other's rescue (Zaidi and Schuler, 1962). As a matter of fact my case studies suggest that the village factions prosper in direct relationship to the prosperity of the villagers in general.

Case studies of the factions were collected, from several villages, through the interview method, by a number of student trainees. Both leaders and ordinary farmers were interviewed. These cases are presented as a part of my general discussion of the problems of the East Pakistan rural society, but first to make a statement regarding factions in the village social organization as a sociological phenomenon.

Factions, as a sociological phenomenon, may be defined as subgroups obtaining in a community comprising persons with similar interests who may have a relationship of implicit or overt conflict with members of other subgroups, similarly constituted, in the same community. Factions obviously presuppose the existence of two or more subgroups in a community. While they may play a positive role in terms of providing cohesion and unity in a subgroup, in general their basis, as observed in East Pakistan, appears to be negative. Observations also indicate that, although factions may have a fairly long duration, they are in no way permanent, and may even shift their focus of interest within a generation.

Village factions are a closed and well-knit group where the frontiers are jealously guarded from encroachment by other factional groups in the community. The leaders of each faction have nothing to do with those of other factions, and social relations among members of two different factions are at a minimum, although it may vary from village to village and from faction to faction. And although factional hostility persists, because of the intradependence of village life, members of opposing factions occasionally must overlook their differences and work closely together for their mutual interests, especially in times of natural calamity.

East Pakistan factions are both leader based and situation based. The clear differentiation Morris (1957) found in Uganda is not found here. As Pocock (1957) points out, when we speak of factions we have in mind conflicting and disrupting groups, or parts, of a whole. They are composite interest groups secondary in nature to kin and lineage. They last as long as the particular interest and the circumstances relating to the potential conflict persist.

Factions have been observed widely as a feature of the rural social structure both in India and in Pakistan. In Pakistan, a British civilian, by the name of Darling, found that factions existed in about 75 per cent of the villages in the Punjab (Inayatullah, 1958). Barth (1959) has discussed factions among Pathans in the northwest frontiers of West Pakistan. In East Pakistan also hardly a village can be found without some old or incipient faction. Often heterogenous elements combine to form a faction because of a mutual interest. The following may be suggested as the reasons behind the development of factions in East Pakistan.

For example, certain families leave the village, acquire wealth, and return. Such families pose a continuing challenge to the prestige and leadership of the old and traditionally respected village families. Any situation presenting a test of leadership between these families or individual members could cause a conflict. The old family, which has long enjoyed the confidence and leadership of the village, will try to minimize the influence and prestige of the new rich family; the newly rich family will attempt to buy the support and friendship of the influential villagers, the result sometimes being a divided village.

Or a village leader may want a public institution—such as a mosque, a school, or a dispensary—to be built in front of his house, and other influential villagers might group together against him.

Factions may also develop because the *imam* of the mosque is seen associating more with a particular group of people in the village and thus unwittingly alienating himself from the rest of the villagers, who may show their dissatisfaction by finding fault with the *imam* and attempting to replace him with another person who would be in their debt for getting him the job. Sometimes, if the opposing group cannot oust the *imam*, they build a new mosque and bring in an *imam* to their liking.

Then a man may be given a sentence for a misdemeanor that some villagers consider excessive while others think it fair; or there may be a clash between members of the same family—particularly concerning a marriage or divorce—that results in a split of the entire village population.

Of course, there are always political disagreements, especially in regard to the Union Council or cooperative elections.

The qualities required for a faction leader are the same as those required for the general village leadership; namely, age, size of one's landholding, eloquence, literacy, outside contacts, family traditions, and devotion and loyalty to the cause of the faction. However, leadership in the faction is generally catalytic because there is more social equality among members of a faction than there would be in the village or community leadership.

The following three cases of village factions reveal the nature, the dynamics, and the interactional patterns obtaining.

**Case 1**

This village is situated about three miles from Comilla on the Daudkandi road. It has 350 families, and a population of about 2,500. Traditionally, it has been a village with Hindu leadership. The majority of the population is still Hindu. There are 100 Muslim and 250 Hindu families out of which about 200

families are of the scheduled caste. Before 1947 one family of
Dewan, known as Dewan Bari, was the acknowledged leader
of the village. Although they have fallen into hard times, they
still command respect in the village, and both Muslims and
Hindus recognize their past family prestige. There are a few
other caste Hindu families. The present case relates to one
Brahmin family and a member of the scheduled caste.

The village is slightly more advanced than other similar
villages. About 60 per cent of its population are literate. There
is a primary school with about two hundred children. There are
two *madrasah*s, two mosques, and two temples in the village.
The main occupation of the villagers is agriculture; but many
of them also engage in subsidiary occupations like bamboo
basket-making, mat-making, or a job in town.

The simple people of the village, as has been noted earlier,
depend very much on the *sirdar*s and *maatbar*s. They seek their
advice in all matters. The group of *maatbar*s often constitute
themselves into a court, and settle petty cases of conflict among
villagers. This village had a similar situation about twenty-five
years ago. The Dewan Bari family had the *sirdar*, who informally
managed village affairs with the help of the *maatbar*s. But the
people lost confidence in them because of their personal involvement with petty village factions and differences.

The present faction involves a disagreement within a
Brahmin family:

Govind, aged seventy, had seven brothers, four of whom died
and two of whom migrated to India. The present case relates
to his brother's widow, Bimla, and his daughter, Ranibala, who
was a minor at the time of the death of her father. Govind
was looking after the property of his widowed sister-in-law
and the niece. Sometime ago, Bimla felt dissatisfied with
Govind's management of her land and took it away and gave
it to one of Govind's cousins on the basis of sharecropping.
After about five years the cousins also dissatisfied her, and
Bimla gave the land to a number of people, one after the other,
until at the time of this study, the land was under the management of Manohar, a member of the scheduled caste. This
situation is the background of the conflict within this family.

The actual faction in this Brahmin family centers around the social conduct of Bimla and her daughter Ranibala, who is now twenty-five years old.

Ranibala was married to Nalini Chatterjee, who has now settled in India. Ranibala went to India with her husband, and had two sons, who are living with their father. About five years ago, Bimla being probably very much dissatisfied with the management of her property, went to India to her daughter. She reportedly found her daughter very unhappy with her husband. She, therefore, decided to bring Ranibala back with her to East Pakistan. Ranibala, after some resistance, agreed and came back to this village with her mother.

Back in the village, Bimla got in touch with Sachindra, another member of the scheduled caste, and a painter in Comilla. Frequent contacts between Bimla and Sachindra developed into an emotional understanding. Sachindra became the unofficial guardian of the family, and started frequenting Bimla's house at any time of the day or night. Rumors of illicit relations between Ranibala and Sachindra began.

Govind and others tried to check Bimla and reprimanded Ranibala. They tried to persuade the mother and daughter to stop meeting Sachindra. Members of the scheduled caste similarly persuaded Sachindra to stop going to Bimla's house. All this was to no avail. Instead, Bimla accused Govind and other members of the family of harrassment. The village *salis* (arbiters in a dispute) assembled in Bimla's house, but since the real matters were not in the open, they went away without reaching a decision. The village was thus divided for and against Bimla. Members of the family, to protect the family name, tried to persuade Ranibala to go back to her husband in India. Bimla would, however, not let her be persuaded. All else failing, members of the family reported to the police that Ranibala was staying illegally in Pakistan, since she was an Indian national. They, therefore, requested the Pakistan authorities to deport her to India. The situation was now seriously developing into a faction, because there were villagers on both sides. The police arrested Ranibala and brought charges of illegal residence against her. Bimla had some of the village *maatbar*s testify in court that Ranibala was a Pakistan national. There was some discrepancy between the name appearing in the passport and the name by which the case was filed. Giving her the benefit of the doubt, the magistrate acquitted Ranibala. After this victory, Bimla and Ranibala openly defied their Brahmin family, with Bimla stating that Govind wanted to usurp the land whose management she had taken away from him.

The present position of the case is that Ranibala continues to meet Sachindra, who now has a part of the village on his side. The family of Govind is disappointed, and has apparently given up Bimla as a lost cause. They have, however, boycotted her from their community. But Bimla does not seem to care. The village remains divided.

## Case 2

This is a predominantly Muslim village, although the pattern of leadership and the general life situation is the same as in the village described above. This village is also adjacent to the town, and is divided into three sections: north, south, and middle.

This village has certain features which are still new in the context of East Pakistan village life. It is quite near the town. It has suffered from the effects of World War II. Most of its land was taken away during the war for the purpose of constructing an aerodrome. Before the war the villagers had sufficient land, and were financially well off. They had to leave their homes and came back only after the war was over. Another feature that sets this village apart is that it has a women's cooperative society, managed entirely by the village women, which, in itself, is a significant development. The village has more than one dozen matriculates, which is considered good by village standards. There are two graduates. There is a teashop, and one ration shop. It has, therefore, as much urban influence as any other village in East Pakistan.

The village has 1,191 people. It has one *madrasah,* five mosques, and one dispensary run by a locally trained doctor. The women's cooperative society runs a consumer shop and an adult education group for women, training them in needlework, toymaking, pottery, and tailoring. The general villagers, however, are not very literate, the percentage being only about 15. The village, in general, is midway between old conservatism and modern progressivism.

The faction which is being described below is basically an expression of the conflict between the old and the new ways of life. A few people in the village have taken up the new way of life, and are trying to instill this same attitude in others. The few old ones are trying to resist and are creating obstacles. The faction may be an indication of the dynamics of resisting social change in a traditionally conservative social structure. There, however, seems to be evidence that the new ways are dominating the thinking of the neutral villagers. Some of them are showing interest in the improved methods of agriculture, and their number is increasing gradually.

There are two leading families of *mir* and *qazi* in the village, the rest are poor Muslims with no pretensions for leadership. The present dispute has a long and complicated history, and a few recent incidents have served as the precipitating causes of the faction between these two leading families. There are a number of prominent villagers on each side, and for one reason or another, they want the crisis to linger on.

The history of the dispute dates back to a legal dispute between the families of Yusuf and Ashu. Yusuf's son was married to the daughter of Ainuddin, son of Ashu *sirdar*. Since Ainuddin had no male issue, the property went to the daughter and thus to Yusuf's son, Ramzan. But a nephew of Ainuddin, Nawab, also had designs on his uncle's property. A lawsuit was lodged by Nawab, who won the case in terms of the Muslim law of inheritance. Thus was begun the incipient faction situation in the village. Ramzan's brother, Hasan, who is seventy-five and a leader because of his age and experience, has never forgiven Nawab.

In addition to the above dispute, there is a history of dispute between the Qazi and Mir families of the village. Originally the leadership of the village was in the Mir family. There was intermarriage between the two families, and as a result Ahmad Mir and Abdul Qazi were cousins. Ahmad Mir on his deathbed declared that Abdul Qazi would be the leader after him, and placed his minor son under the protection of Abdul Qazi. Thus the leadership was transferred to the Qazi family. The minor son, even after reaching his majority, accepted the wishes of his father and obeyed Abdul Qazi; but his son, Siraj Mir, does not accept this transfer made by his grandfather and wants to reclaim the leadership of the village. His counterpart in the Qazi family is Sona Mia Qazi, who is the leader. Thus there is bad blood between Siraj Mir and Sona Mia Qazi.

The leaders of the present faction are Hasan, Akbar, and Sona Mia Qazi in one party; and Nawab, supported by Siraj Mir and Sikander, in the other. The following incidents worked as the immediate causes of the dispute, which divided the village. These groups will now be referred to by the first letter of the leader's name, i.e., *S* and *N*. Group *S* is ideologically more conservative, glorifying the past and adhering to the traditional way of life. Group *N* is enlightened, progressive, and willing to experiment with new ideas. Group *N* has, therefore, managed to gain the sympathy and moral support of the officials involved in cooperative and community development programs.

Four recent incidents have served to heighten the tension between the factional groups.

First, a boy of twelve was taking a bath in a tank belonging to Akbar. When Akbar's brother, Altaf, told the boy to get out of the tank, the boy did not obey. Altaf got angry, and beat the boy. The father of the boy complained to the village leaders and arranged a *salis* of the *maatbars* for a decision of the case. The *salis* decided against Altaf, who did not accept the decision. Altaf has been boycotted by the village. But he is a brother of Akbar, belonging to the *S* group. Altaf, on his own, has aligned with the leader of *S*, who is related to him.

Second, in a village marriage arranged entirely by *S*, the *N* group was not consulted. It was also decided by group *S* not to invite group *N*. The father of the girl did not agree to this omission, however. The two groups came to the ceremony, but *N* felt slighted. There was a hot exchange of words. *S* was accused of associating with Altaf in spite of his boycott by the villagers. The quarrel increased, and both groups left in anger.

Third, the local Union Council sanctioned a small sum of money for the repair of a village road. Mafiz, a supporter of group *S*, had encroached on the road. When the repair was to start, Mafiz appealed to group *S* for help. They took this opportunity to annoy group *N*, who wanted the road repaired. The matter has been referred to the chairman of the Union Council. No decision has yet been taken.

Fourth, an incident that relates to the women's cooperative society, of which Nawab's wife is the cashier. Some six months ago the cooperative obtained washing soda from the government at a subsidized price. Before a decision on the selling price of the soda was made, the chairman of the society had to go away on personal business. It was, therefore, decided by the secretary that, pending a decision on the selling price, soda would be sold at the rate of *Rs.* 1/8 (30 cents) per *seer* (about two pounds), and the amount would be adjusted against the consumers when the final price was decided upon. With this understanding, soda was sold to a villager. The villager returned the soda saying that the price was 50 per cent higher than the market price. He did not agree with the explanation about the temporary pricing, and lodged a case to the anticorruption police. The police came, seized the records, and closed the shop. A case had started. Since Nawab's wife was associated with the cooperative, Sona Mia had a perfect opportunity to side wholeheartedly with the complainant. He openly started his tirade against the women's cooperative society and against Nawab as a supporter of the society.

The case against the cooperative has been withdrawn, but the seeds of discord have been sown. Nawab cannot forget the insult to him and his wife, in which Sona Mia so actively participated against him.

This is the case in which personal wrongs, family prestige, conflict of the village leadership, and a clash between old and new ways of life are all tied together. The new ways will possibly triumph ultimately, but the other forces are likely to exist for some time to come.

## Case 3

This village has a mixed Hindu and Muslim population of about 1,800 people. Until about two decades ago, the entire village accepted the leadership and the social authority of the Zamindar family. The Zamindar family was rich and always ready to help the villagers in emergencies. The family had been the leader of the village for about one century.

Under the leadership of the Zamindar family the villagers started a Village Cooperative Society, a joint venture of the village that ran a free dispensary, organized adult education classes, and engaged in other social welfare activities.

The position changed with the Zamindar family's loss of landed property. The family became poorer, and could not maintain the same standard of living and helping the needy villagers. And because the family was not educated, they fell on evil days. Unfortunately, the members of the Zamindar family made alliances with certain newly rich families in the village who were not respected by the villagers. The villagers thought them to be upstarts who had acquired wealth but were not deserving of equal status with the Zamindar family.

The villagers lost respect for the Zamindar family because of their unholy alliance with these newly-rich families, who hoped to acquire the respect and good will of the people merely on the strength of their wealth, which was an insult to village traditions and led to hostility against these families and also against those who allied with them, thus establishing two factions.

There are two major factions and one small minority subgroup trying to remain neutral but sympathizing with one of the major groups in the faction. The important subgroup and also the basis of the faction is the group of families which acquired wealth through brokerage and aspired toward village leadership. Since these families had no previous family prestige in the village, they tried to acquire it through marriage into the Zamindar family. Thus they have involved the Zamindar family on their side, which has, in turn, made the villagers hostile to the Zamindar family. The marriage alliance, instead of giving prestige to the newly rich families, alienated both themselves and the Zamindar family. The members of this subgroup have also other weaknesses that the villagers do not like. They are arrogant, and according to the villagers, dishonest. Some of them have also acquired a bad name because of their loose moral character.

The other group in the faction comprises the majority of the village farmers who are neither rich nor powerful enough to meet the first group in the open. They have mainly been ignoring the Zamindars and the other allied families, and refuse to acknowledge them as village leaders.

The third and seemingly neutral group consists of a few educated and enlightened persons. They are teachers and professionals. They are respected by the farmers for their education, but they are too disinterested in village affairs to be of much use either to the first group or to the second.

The group of village farmers has not reconciled with the idea of accepting families with low beginnings as leaders. They do not consider them better than themselves. This is the psychological dilemma of village farmers.

This situation is typical of many village factions in East Pakistan. Owing to recent economic activities many villages have witnessed the emergence of poor families as economically solvent families. With this newly acquired wealth has come a clash for leadership between the traditionally aristocratic family and the newly rich. It has also led to value conflict between traditional agrarian and modern urban values. The resolution of this conflict alone will lead to resolution of the factions because, in cases like this, the causes are not concrete and touch upon the deeper layers of the rural culture.

The phenomenon of factions, as should be apparent now, is fairly common in our villages. A fact that is brought out by the cases presented above is that the factions are very closely related to the value structure and the attitudinal configuration of the villagers. Very often factions develop because someone has unwittingly or unknowingly violated or deviated from some of the social norms and attitudes. In almost all villages certain families have traditionally had leadership status; others have looked up to them for help, guidance, and advice. The moment someone questions or acts in a way prejudicial to their accepted status, the seeds of an incipient faction are planted.

Another fact that stands out in the case studies is that social changes and the requirements for readjustments in behavior patterns are likely to initiate factions, and that the change agents working for the development of the villages ought to realize the importance of psychological adjustment and the fact that any change affecting the equilibrium of community life in traditional societies is strongly resisted. Introduction of any change in the established pattern of sociocultural behavior requires a prior knowledge of the interpersonal relationships and the village loyalties and affiliations. It also requires a sympathetic understanding of the villagers' scale of values, their prejudices and stereotypes, and the local pattern of authority.

A third factor that may be relevant in this connection is the nature of the groupings that emerge in the factions. In the context of Muslim society and particularly in East Pakistan, as has been pointed out earlier, social classification is flexible and fluid because of the general economic deprivation all over the rural sector. There are no big landlords and their tenants, neither is there much evidence of a permanent dominant class in terms of the Indian "dominant" caste (Srinivas, 1959). There is also evidence to show that in many faction-ridden villages members of the same kinship groups belong to different factions. It is, therefore, suggested that although kinship relations play an important part in most factions, the group loyalties are also determined by economic and political considerations.

A further delineation from the case studies appears to be the personality as well as the sociopolitical and economic standing of the faction leaders. This is an area about which very little systematic information is available. I have not come across any study of the personality of village or faction leaders, and most generalizations about such leaders are based on impressionistic and out-of-context observations. Studies of village leaders may require intensive investigations of a whole range of persons or the Lewinian model of "social climates" may serve as a frame of reference (Barker, *et al.*, 1941). This area has generally been overlooked even in studies of Indian villages conducted with American resources. My own resources were much too meager for planning such a large-scale study.

A working hypothesis concerning the nature and genesis of factionalism has been suggested by Siegel and Beals (1960), in which they suggest that factionalism is a reproducible phenomenon and does not depend upon a particular period of history. It can occur whenever groups of a certain kind encounter external pressures of a certain kind, and upon the particular pattern of strain within the community. This condition they designate as "pervasive factionalism," and illustrate it by two cases selected from India and Taos Pueblo. "Factionalism" is defined as "overt conflict within a group which leads to the increasing abandonment of cooperative activities." This approach seems promising, and as the authors claim, can be tested in any culture or society and in any kind of subgroup. They hope that it will be possible to produce or eliminate the phenomena associated with factionalism at will.

# CHAPTER VI

# RITUALS, SUPERSTITIONS, AND FATALISTIC BELIEFS

FATALISM generally refers to a ready and uncritical explanation of a phenomenon in terms of the doings of unknown agent or agents. It is characterized by a rigid belief in the Supernatural and a passive dependence on Nature's taking her own course. Fatalism may be both an individual and a group phenomenon; and more often than not, it has historical and cultural origins (Spiro, 1966). It is generally assumed that groups with feelings of insecurity and helplessness owing to the absence of facilities for controlling natural mishaps show greater fatalistic tendencies because, psychologically perhaps, it absolves them of any responsibility for their failures and frustrations. It also sustains them against natural calamities and unexpected happenings (Kerr, 1963).

It is generally believed that simple village people in almost all developing countries are fatalistic in their attitude to the Supernatural and the Unseen. These attitudes have a strong religious bias. It is because of this easy credulity of the villagers in East Pakistan that the simple religious tenets have become mixed up with a number of rituals and ceremonies with the result that, in many cases, the genuine religion has been relegated to a secondary position. Fatalistic beliefs and associated superstitions have acquired deep religious significance. The East Pakistan villager is a typical example of a religious man who strongly believes in the divinity of all unexplainable events.

There are, it seems, two different levels of their religion for all villagers: besides the official Islam or Hinduism with their prescribed practices, injunctions, and beliefs, there is the Unknown Agent responsible for floods, droughts, diseases, and epidemics. The villager, whether a Hindu or a Muslim, has to keep "it" happy and satisfied; and to forestall "its" evil designs through some preventive act, small sacrifice, prayers, and visits to holy men and places.

A similar situation has been observed in Burma, a country very near our scene of study, but very different in its official religion. To quote:

... these two religious systems (in Burma), the official Buddhism and the unformalised religion of the NATS are the basis of the concepts about health and illness, misfortune, well-being, potency and achievement. ... If he suffered misfortune it was because he had failed in his preventive measures against the NATS, or because he had unwittingly offended them. (Mead, 1955)

In East Pakistan and in other Muslim communities of Pakistan and India, fatalism and superstitions have clearly historical and sociocultural bases. Primarily, it may have developed out of the deep religiosity of the people and also possibly because of the prevailing traditions of pseudomystical beliefs, reinforced by the influence of a class of mendicants who, in order to retain their "invisible" leadership, wish to perpetuate the attitude of indifference and prejudice against modern technological tools and skills.

Fatalism in a community, therefore, is a function of the socioeconomic structure of its group life, which becomes internalized as a part of the individual's belief system. Religion may provide the anchor for most of the beliefs and attitudes in the East, but the objects and forces one believes in are not isolated from the workaday life of the individuals in the community. The rural society in East Pakistan, where this study was conducted, is typical of the so-called developing societies in regard to its beliefs, attitudes, and prejudices.

Based on the foregoing remarks, it was assumed that the majority of the villagers in East Pakistan are fatalistic in their attitudes and approach to natural calamities and supernatural forces; and that fatalism is common to both Hindus and Muslims, although the basic tenets of their religions differ greatly. An attempt was made to find out some of the attitudes toward various occasions in their lives involving a tendency to superstitious beliefs and fatalistic prejudices.

Our study indicated that 99 per cent of the Muslims and 98 per cent of the Hindus responding believe that man has no control over his means of livelihood, and that God assigns it to him. To the East Pakistani villagers man is a helpless creature, unable even to procure his livelihood unless God wills so. They are resigned to Fate, and will not believe that any man could change what has already been ordained for him. As far as this attitude toward predetermined causation is concerned, there is no difference between the Muslim and the Hindu villagers. They are rigid in this belief and, therefore, are usually indifferent and even apathetic to making efforts for the improvement of their situation. They have a dim view of the effectiveness of their own efforts. An enlightened or educated man explaining to them the benefits of self-help and individual efforts for the improvement of their economic conditions might likely be dubbed as an irreligious man or an infidel. They exhibit the same fatalistic attitudes not only in matters of economic improvement but also in affairs relating to disease.

When someone in the family falls ill, the first and most spontaneous reaction of a villager is to pray to God for his recovery. This is, of course, a general reaction of many people in danger or trouble. Besides, the villagers are not generally opposed to calling a doctor. The point of emphasis, however, in this regard is the greater faith in the efficacy of prayer as against medicine. Often if the patient is cured, the credit for the recovery goes to the *maulvi* who offered the prayer for the ill and not to the doctor's medicine. In fact, it is this half-educated *maulvi* who is generally responsible for reinforcing the villagers' belief in their own incompetence, and here the *maulvi*s have a vested interest in not letting the villagers get too enlightened because then they would not listen to the *maulvi*s or depend upon their blessings.

For warding off diseases and epidemics, the responses indicated that they are willing to call a doctor (which in many cases may be beyond the means of the poor villager), a *hakim*, or a *kabiraj*. These two professional people mentioned last represent the Greek and Ayurvedic systems of medicine, respectively. However, they are not ignoring the *maulvi* and prayer to God. The villagers would also go to a religious man and have him blow his breath, with some silent recitations, on a jar of water, which is then taken by the patient. This water is known as *pani-para*, and is believed to effect a cure because of its having now been blessed. The Hindu respondents are more frequently willing to put their faith in the doctor and his medicine. During epidemics, however, the rituals performed are characteristically religious and collective.

There have been recent attempts to propagate the idea of birth control and family planning in East Pakistan villages. The greatest resistance that has been put against this program relates to the villagers' fatalistic faith that births and deaths cannot be controlled by human effort. In the responses of the villagers, it was indicated that 83 per cent of the Muslims and 85 per cent of the Hindus believe that the number of children in the family cannot be controlled. The villagers, therefore, do not believe in preventive measures, and may even feel that any attempt to control birth is an act against God. They believe in God's will, which is always beneficient and for the good of man.

This deep faith in the will of God has, unfortunately, been extended to beliefs in the efficacy of prayer and the blessings of saints and holy men. There are three aspects to the belief in saints and holy men: the person himself (*peer*), the grave of the saint where people assemble occasionally or annually in a sort of fair (*urs*), and objects blessed by the holy man, generally in the form of verses of the Holy Qur'ān or incantations on a piece of paper written by the holy man (a *taviz*), which the individual wears on his person to ward off evil spirits. The general belief is that a holy person, or saint, possesses a sort of blessing, or blessed virtue, from God in his person. This possession is termed *barkat*. The belief is genuine, but the later distortions of the concept have led many imposters to claim *barkat* for themselves; and the poor villagers, too ready to believe, would shudder to doubt such a claim.

Generally, the belief is that the more pious a person is, the more efficacious is the *barkat* issuing forth from his person or his words. The villagers believe that such *barkat* will help them against all dangers, provide them relief from pain, rid them of disease, save them from ghosts and other evil spirits, keep them safe from snake bite, and may even give them a child if the wife is known to be sterile. Thus there is a *taviz* containing *barkat* for every occasion, written by a *peer*, or saint. Sometimes villagers go long distances to visit a *peer* and to obtain a *taviz* written by him.

The shrines, the venue for the *urs*, of all important and pious *peers*, possess immense *barkat*. They are protected and preserved and new monuments may be erected on the grave of the saint. Both Hindus and Muslims visit such shrines and present their offerings of money and gifts to the caretakers of the shrines. In return for these gifts, they may get some sweets alleged to possess *barkat*. It is also believed that a holy saint never really dies; and, therefore, the villager believes that his supplications would be listened to by the saint who would then respond from the grave in terms of fulfilling his wish. It may be added here that orthodox Islam treats such beliefs as heresies.

The respondents indicated their desire to possess amulets, although the majority of them, both Hindus and Muslims, did not have any on their person, for the reason that they could not secure one for themselves. The responses also revealed that all the Hindu respondents and 36 per cent of the Muslims have gone to an *urs*. The Hindus went there to hear sermons; and for the few Muslims, the purpose was *ziarat* (the sight of the holy man or his tomb, or grave). It is a curious fact that the Hindus do not discriminate between Hindu and Muslim saints.

Most of the villagers who visit these holy places believe that it helps them in some way. It gives them peace of mind, which makes them brood less on their troubles. Some thought their desires were fulfilled as a result of their visit. Some, however, could not verbalize their satisfaction, but confessed that it had helped them in general.

Another expression of their belief in the efficacy of prayer and the limitations of man's control of nature is their attitude to scientific medicine. They firmly believe that if a man is going to die, no medicine can save him. There may be more factual than fatalistic content in such a belief; but the effects of such a belief may result in an out and out lack of effort to save someone who obviously is dying, but could probably still be saved. The belief implies that one may not even care to apply medicine if he believes that the patient is going to die anyway. This weakens the concept that one must not give up hope until the last minute.

Villagers believe strongly in the Supernatural, and invoke the mercy of these forces whenever they are in danger or feel that all worldly means of help and support have been exhausted. Then they resort to prayers. In matters of disease, floods, and other natural calamities connected with agricultural operations, they perform a number of ritualistic ceremonies implying their superstitious beliefs in the Unseen. The nature of the prayer and the ceremony may be different for different cultural and religious groups. The East Pakistani Muslim villagers, with whose behavior I am particularly familiar, have a number of ways of praying to God for relief. One of the most important is a prayer for rain. When the monsoon is late, people assemble in the field and offer a special prayer. The *maulvi* will probably tell them that there is too much sinning in the village, and, therefore, the rains have been withheld. The people standing in the scorching heat implore and wail to God to drop his mercy (rain) on sinful mankind. There are more prayers if the rain does not come with the first assembly.

After the rains come, the cultivators go to prepare the field for sowing. Before the sowing they normally consult the Hindu calendar for a propitious day to begin. Besides lack of rain, the cultivator is also disturbed by too much rain, or floods. Again, locusts may appear or a cyclone may come to destroy the crop. In all such cases the villagers' only recourse is the *maulvi* or the *pundit* (a Hindu priest), who comes to help after extorting money and a feast, and after exhorting him for both committed and uncommitted sins.

Another expression of deep religiosity in Muslims, especially on occasions of helplessness and desperation, is to arrange for a *meelad* which, when performed strictly in the true religious spirit, means a gathering in which the life and character of the Prophet of Islam are described by the *maulvi*, who may be invited especially for the occasion. In East Pakistan such occasions are the month of *Ramadan* (Fasting), new harvest, the birth of a son, and in connection with any calamity endangering the crops. The Hindus also have similar ceremonies (*Puja* festivals) on many occasions similar to those of the Muslims. However, it may be added that *meelad* very rarely is arranged in the true religious spirit. It is more often as a penance, or a gesture of thankfulness to God, but the *maulvis* make it an occasion for profit. Without being unfair to *maulvis*, one may say that most of them in the villages in East Pakistan are only semiliterate. Their knowledge of religion is based more on hearsay than on genuine learning. Most of them cannot even correctly pronounce the Arabic words, the language of many of their citations in the *meelad*. But, unfortunately for the villagers in East Pakistan, they are the only persons who are supposed to know religion. This situation, therefore, has led to a mixing of religion with superstitions, folklore, and fatalistic beliefs.

I once had occasion to go to a *meelad* in a village. It was a big gathering, with people coming from a number of villages. The occasion was the celebration for the new harvest. Two *maulvis* spoke. They recited Persian and Arabic verses. One could see that they were not doing it correctly, but for the villagers every word they uttered was the word of God and the Prophet. In many cases thus, the *maulvis* have taken advantage of the ignorance of the village people, and have exploited them for their own profit.

In response to our questions, we found that both Muslims and Hindus always depend on religion as the last resort. Only 15 per cent of them said that their dependence was greater in times of danger. None of the respondents, however, was clear about how religion had helped him. There is possibly a very strong belief that all success and achievement, in the last analysis, are owing to faith in God. No villager—Muslim or Hindu— would ever, for a moment, feel that religion could not help him.

These beliefs and rituals play a very important role in the group life of East Pakistani villagers. Most of their social and cultural prejudices and attitudes can be explained in terms of these beliefs, which have a long history. It is both a history of their toils and a history of their tribulations against the forces of recurrent calamities, as well as a part of their cultural heritage derived from misrepresented pseudomystical sayings of great saints and reformers.

There is, however, reason to believe that this general fatalism has been changing during the last few decades, possibly owing to industrialization and urban influences. In certain cases we found less fatalism than was expected of a village population in East Pakistan. Some of these changes will be indicated by responses to other questions discussed in later chapters.

In replies to many of the questions there was no evidence of any basic difference between the Hindus and the Muslims. This fact supports my view that there are historical and socio-cultural origins of fatalism, and that the differences of religious affiliations play a very marginal role in the formation of fatalistic attitudes. The following facts may suggest an explanation for this similarity, despite a bitter history of Hindu-Muslim tension in the subcontinent.

In the Pak-Indian subcontinent, many Hindus have faith in Muslim saints and holy men. In certain parts, Hindus wear amulets given by Muslim *faqeers* (mendicants). Reciprocally, many Muslims in the rural areas respect and revere Hindu *sadhus* (those who have renounced the world).

Many Muslim rituals have, in general, been influenced by those of the Hindus, and vice versa. The common attitude, therefore, is a direct result of the process of intergroup fusion and assimilation, which has gone on for many centuries.

The devastating effects of natural calamities hit the two communal groups with equal severity, and the stresses of life compel them to bury their differences and make similar and often collective efforts to seek remedies.

We have described some family ceremonies in the last chapter. Some other significant rituals and ceremonies have been described earlier in this chapter. Perhaps some of the most popular superstitious beliefs and rituals will be of interest.

## Agricultural Rituals

At the beginning of the sowing season, Muslim farmers invite a *maulvi* and Hindu farmers invite a *pundit* to perform some prayers and give religious blessings to assure a successful harvest. At the time of reaping the harvest, they arrange for a feast with friends and relatives at which, also, the *maulvi* or the *pundit* may be invited. This feast is known as *na-banna* in certain districts.

There are some other Muslim practices borrowed from the Hindus. One of these is the occasion when a new cow is bought. The female members of the household receive the cow with candlelight, rice seed, and grass; and like the Hindus, they also put a red sign on her forehead.

Cultivators do not sow seeds or transplant saplings on Tuesdays or Saturdays. These two days are considered to be inauspicious for sowing. The first harvesting is done either on a Thursday or Friday. *140926*

No farmer will cut down his bamboo trees on Sunday (*Rabi-var*) and Thursday (*Bishat-var*), the belief being that the bamboo shoots will be destroyed by *raba poka* and *bish poka* (insects associated with the names of these two days).

While sowing the seed for the jack-fruit tree, the villager will sweeten his mouth with sugar or molasses, and carry the seeds in a big pot. He believes that by so doing the tree will grow big in size, and the fruit will be sweet.

When the paddy is infested with insects, the cultivators get blessed water from a *maulvi* and sprinkle it in the field in the hope of killing the insects. They also place earthenwares painted with lime on bamboo poles in the hope of saving their crop from an evil eye.

The farmer believes that if anyone puts oil on his head and then touches fruit-bearing trees or plants, the growth of the plant will be retarded. When paddy ripens, he takes some ears of paddy and hangs a bunch of it in his house, believing that this procedure will increase the yield. There is another belief of the farmer that associates a good paddy crop with a good mango crop, and heavy floods with abundant growth of tamarind.

### Superstitious Sayings

Some superstitious sayings, believed both by Muslims and by Hindus in rural communities, are:

If an owl hoots at night when a person is lying ill in the house, it is believed that the person will soon die.

When a person dreams that some of his teeth have fallen out, or his mosquito net has caught fire, it is believed that some members of his family will die.

If dogs howl at night during a general epidemic, it is feared that the epidemic may break out in that particular area.

At a time of severe cyclone and storm, if *Azaan* (call for prayer) is recited loudly and repeatedly, the fury of the wind will die down.

During a serious cattle epidemic or in a human epidemic of cholera or smallpox, one's house will become inaccessible to evil spirits if he posts one bamboo pole at each corner of the house.

While embarking on a journey, if a villager sees an empty jar or a country boat on dry land, he should break his journey, come back, and start again.

The first sight in the morning of a barren woman is considered inauspicious to begin a day.

If a married woman dreams of fruit, she will bear a child in the near future; if she dreams of eating fruit, she will remain childless.

When a certain bird, called *kutum pankhi,* sings on one's roof, or a utensil falls from one's hand, it is an indication that a guest is coming to his house.

When one's palm itches, it indicates that he will receive money from some unexpected source.

When one's sole itches, it indicates that he will undertake a long journey.

If after someone makes a statement a lizard "ta-ta's," it is believed that the statement is correct.

A quarrel will occur between two people if one takes salt out of the other's plate, or if he picks some lime from the finger of the other person. (Lime is taken with betel leaves, to which the villagers are generally addicted.)

## What One Should and Should Not Do

Do not comb your hair at night or look in a mirror because your life will be shortened, and you will become poor.

Do not sweep the floor or throw away the used water at night, for the family may become poor.

Do not cut your nails or hair at night, for you may become poor.

When a child breaks his baby teeth, he should deposit them in a rat hole; for by so doing he will cause fine, sharp, and even teeth to grow.

Do not cross over or walk over a person who is lying down because it will stop his growth.

While taking food sitting on the floor, do not spread your legs because then you will be married at a very distant place.

During examination time, do not eat eggs or utter the word *kechap* (tortoise) or look at an empty pitcher because any of these acts will mean your failure at the examination.

If you start on an errand with a definite purpose in mind but you are uncertain how best to accomplish it and someone from behind sneezes, you should stay back in the house and wait for some time before going out again, otherwise you will never succeed in your mission.

## Popular Supernatural Beliefs

There is a wide range of popular beliefs among the villagers about supernatural beings living around the community unseen (Karim, 1955). These beliefs, besides being strong motivational forces in social behavior, indicate the basic insecurity of life in the village.

One important supernatural being is the *jinn* (geni), now considered a part of the total belief system of the Muslims. There might be a trace of the Hindu concept of the demon in these beliefs. There are literally very few Muslims who do not believe in the existence of the *jinn*, and they are often considered infidels by the *maulvi*. Belief in the existence of the *jinn* stems from evidence in the Qur'ān wherein *jinn* is mentioned as one of the various creations of God; but the exact nature of a *jinn*'s behavior and characteristics stems mainly from superstitions, folklore, and bizarre distortions motivated by a variety of considerations, not the least important of which would be the vested interests of the *maulvi*.

It is believed that there are millions of *jinn*s in the world, as numerous as human beings. However, there are stories about the possession by a *jinn* and the behavior of the possessed. Persons have allegedly been slapped by *jinn*s or roughly handled while they were passing by a lonely place. The only way to avoid molestation by a *jinn* is to recite verses from the Holy Qur'ān. It is believed by all Muslims that the verses of the Qur'ān scare away all evil spirits, and even the *jinn* is expected to respect a Muslim who reads it.

The favorite haunting places of the *jinn* are a lonely graveyard, a mosque, marshy land, deserted human habitation, the crossing of two roads, and certain types of large trees. These places are locally known as *khal*s. Persons must be careful while passing by these *khal*s, especially during the night. It is advised that a person recite some verses of the Qur'ān and no harm will come to him. Women are strongly advised against passing by the side of the *khal* without covering their head. Women must not use too much perfume. They are especially to be careful during their menstrual period. It is also believed that *jinn*s love young and beautiful girls and, therefore, they are advised to take an old woman with them while going out.

If a *jinn* gets possession of a woman, the *ojha* (sorcerer) is called for help. He is supposed to be more powerful in relation to the *jinn* than the *maulvi*, because it is assumed that one should know more than the Qur'ān to drive away the *jinn*. The *ojha* makes use of Hindu incantations and other mysterious verses. He lights a fire and throws pieces of turmeric and mustard seeds into it, which then give out a peculiar kind of incense. He then invokes all kinds of Hindu gods and goddesses and Muslim saints and holy men. It is believed that the smell of the fire· with these spices is intolerable to the *jinn*. The *ojha* creating the proper psychological atmosphere threatens the invisible *jinn* with dire consequences and asks him to leave at once. The *jinn* holds out many pleas accusing the carelessness of the possessed woman. After threats and counter-threats, the *jinn* yields to the superior powers of the *ojha* and leaves the woman.

*Jinn*s are generally invisible, though at times they may take human form. They are supposed to offer prayers in the mosque, unseen by the people. Muslims allow the *jinn*s to make use of the mosque before they begin their own prayers. It is also believed that there are good and bad beings among *jinn*s, just as there are among humans. *Jinn*s have their own world, and come out in the night. They may sometimes join human groups in human form. The only way to recognize a *jinn* in human form is to look at his feet. They are believed to have horse hoofs, which they cannot change. They also do not cast their shadow.

Besides the *jinn*, there is another class of supernatural beings known as *deo-angshi*, which is not a Muslim being like the *jinn*. It is one of the Hindu ghosts of which the Muslims are also afraid. There are a number of other ghosts and witches in which the villagers believe, but the belief in *deo-angshi* is somewhat different and more significant.

Literally, *"deo-angshi"* means "that which takes the quality of a demon or god," *"deo,"* meaning both god and a demon. Thus a *deo-angshi*, like a *jinn*, may be both good and bad. They live only in lakes and ponds. The bigger the pond, the mightier the *deo-angshi*. In some lakes and bigger ponds small crocodiles, big fish, and other aquatic animals living in the pond might be taken to be *deo-angshi*s. People afraid to offend, offer them food and generally avoid them. However, not all *deo-angshi*s are visible.

The belief in *deo-angshi*s is important because, in East Pakistan, almost every household in the village has a small pond and every village has a number of big and small ponds. Since *deo-angshi*s live only in large ponds, people are afraid to use these ponds for cleansing purposes. If a person does so and a *deo-angshi* is living in the pond, it will appear in his dream and warn him not to do so again. If that person neglects the warning and repeats the behavior, the *deo-angshi* will next time pull him down into the water and he will be drowned.

A general belief about demons, ghosts, *jinn*s, and *deo-angshi*s is that, if someone uses a *khal* tree in constructing a wooden safe (many rich villagers use wooden safes to put their money in) and if the tree was being used by some of these beings, it will walk out of the house to a pond where a *deo-angshi* lives, or it will turn itself into a *deo-angshi*. It is, therefore, said that a wooden safe should not be made of wood from a single tree because it may be the tree infested by ghosts.

These beliefs about supernatural beings and the popular superstitions and fatalistic attitudes of the villagers are a part of the community life in East Pakistan. These beliefs are so important to the villagers that no logic or convincing proof of their falsity will have any effect. The child learns of these beliefs as a part of his cultural conditioning, both at home and in the village, and then internalizes them as a part of his cognitive structure of personality. These beliefs constitute his "inner world of meaning," and determine his behavior in many life situations. We must take these attitudes into account in any understanding of the villager's social behavior.

# CHAPTER VII

# VALUE ORIENTATION

ROBERT REDFIELD (1956), in his book *Peasant Society and Culture*, speaks of the culture of the peasant community as an aspect or dimension of the larger culture of the group of which the community is a part. He speaks of a "little culture," represented by the particular peasant community, and a "greater culture," characterized by something of what goes on in the minds of remote teachers, priests, or philosophers whose thinking affects and perhaps is affected by the peasantry. Thus the peasant culture is likened to a small circle within much larger and less clearly defined areas of culture incorporating the refinements of religion, art, literature, and other higher forms of culture. It is in this light that we should examine the basic value orientation of the East Pakistani villagers.

The value orientation of the East Pakistan village culture is basically Islamic in origin, although it has been modified after centuries of close contact with Hindus. In some cases the two groups have identical rituals and customs. However, they have maintained a basic difference in their attitude toward life.

For the purposes of this study, "basic values" are defined as "matters which one feels are important in his life." The respondents were given a list of propositions which, I assumed, were of some significance in their lives. They were asked to indicate their responses in a three-category answer sheet with *important*, *neutral*, or *not important*. They were also asked to evaluate a person in regard to "if he behaves thus in such and such a situation." These situations were focused on some of the basic value orientations in the life of the villagers, and were used for Muslims and Hindus alike, for it is believed that because of their close association, they would have similar attitudes.

In the Pakistan culture the greatest virtue of a Muslim man or woman is that he or she be a good Muslim. In describing the virtues of a person, we often begin by saying that he or she is a good Muslim. This statement has certain connotations, learned from childhood, which most Pakistanis understand completely.

The Hindus were asked what characteristics are necessary for one to be a good Hindu. Of the fifty-five respondents participating, all agreed that a good Hindu would be a good person, who would think well of others and be reliable. Only one respondent said that a good Hindu is one who has a high family descent. This absence of emphasis on high caste seems significant, and may reflect the influence of the casteless Muslim society. But while cultural interchange exists, Muslims, being highly orthodox in their religious observances, would never accept a modification of their basic and fundamental beliefs. A modification would be acceptable only if it did not violate the basic tenets of the Qur'ān and the *Sunnah*.

In response to the next question regarding the qualifications of a good Hindu woman, the male Hindu respondents of the study emphasized that she should do noble deeds; have good character; and be devoted to husband, to religion, and to parents. Here again the emphasis on high caste is missing, and the moral character of the woman is emphasized. The position of the husband in Hinduism is exalted. The qualities given of a good Hindu woman are quite in line with the Hindu concept of the wife and the daughter. Only one person thought that a good Hindu woman should also be educated. This, however, is not yet a very significant qualification for a woman in our village culture. To the same two questions, Muslim respondents emphasized the performance of religious duties, which alone can make one a good Muslim man or woman. The basic tenets of Islam which a good Muslim, both man and woman, is to follow are the prayers, fasting in *Ramadan,* reciting the verses from the Holy Qur'ān, never telling lies, and possessing good moral character. It is evident that, unlike the Hindu respondents, where the emphasis was on good ethical virtues, the enumeration of good qualities for a Muslim relates primarily to the observance of the Islamic tenets.

Similarly, in response to the question about the virtues of a good Muslim woman, those questioned said that a virtuous woman, according to Islam, should be devoted to the perform-ance of her religious duties, and should have an unimpeachable moral character. She should offer her prayers regularly and fast, should be devoted to the Qur'ān, observe *pardah,* should be of good moral character, should be educated, and should be devoted to her husband and to her parents. Devotion to her husband is an important part of the religious training for a Muslim woman, but the small frequency of responses indicating this virtue is possibly owing to the fact that it is implied in her devotion to religion. The small frequency of devotion to parents may be owing to the fact that the question possibly implied that the answer should be about married women and, therefore, the question of devotion to parents does not arise. Otherwise, it is one of our basic cultural realities that girls are devoted to their parents. As a matter of fact they are more devoted than are the boys, who often flout parental authority on the strength that it is generally tolerated in the male-dominated society.

The analysis of these two questions clearly points to the differences in value orientation based on religion. Muslims all over Pakistan are very greatly influenced by religious injunc-tions in their attitudes and the general cultural conditioning. The training that children receive at home is, to a very large extent, implicitly determined by Islamic rules of conduct and behavior as perceived by their parents. There may be individual variations owing to personal-social conditioning (Young, 1947); but in terms of the general culture-personality approach, Islam is the primary force in the development of the "basic structure of personality" in Pakistan, and more particularly in village Pakistan.

With this background information on the villagers' per-ceptions of a good man and a good woman, both for Hindus and Muslims, we pass on to a detailed account of certain basic values and norms of behavior in the rural society of East

Pakistan. These values and norms, however, are not exclusive to the villagers, but refer to Pakistan society in general. The village, representing the smaller cultural unit, embodies the norms of the larger culture of, not only Pakistan, but the Muslim culture in general.

According to Redfield, the basic peasant values are characterized by an intense attachment to native soil; a reverent disposition toward habitat and ancestral ways; a restraint on individual self-seeking in favor of family and community; a certain suspiciousness, mixed with appreciation, of town life; and a sober and earthy ethic. Although agreeing with him that it is too vague a characterization, I feel that, in general, he is not too much off the mark. These values are quite basic in the life of East Pakistani peasants. There may be numerous explanations of these values in terms of historical and social events influencing the peasants. There may also be some impact of religious attitudes towards the land and family.

There is a general saying in villages which classifies the various occupations into four, in order of their preference and respect: agriculture, trade, service, and beggary. The basic idea of this saying is that a profession or an occupation is respectable only if it does not make one subservient to someone else. It also indicates the prime importance of the possession of land or property which makes one independent and his own master. This is an old saying reminiscent of the days when land yielded more grain than a family could consume and was sufficient to provide for other needs. The pressure of population was less, and people did not have to leave their hearth and home to go looking for jobs. The saying also indirectly indicates a dislike for townspeople because they do not generally engage in agriculture, do not have landed property, and have to depend on service for their living. At the time when this saying may have originated, the concept of trade was also possibly confined to village trades of consumer goods because, obviously, the modern complex of business was unknown. It may, however, be indicated that this concept of the hierarchy of occupations is changing, not because of a change of value orientation particularly, or attitudes to landed property; but most likely because of the recent rapid economic changes which have brought down the scales in favor of the business profession, and have reduced agriculture to a mere subsidiary occupation with no great financial rewards.

The present study reveals, however, that the villagers still retain the basic value orientations of their forefathers. They have not changed much in their attitudes in spite of the drastic changes in the material culture of the society. They still wish to possess landed property, and landless villagers still generally occupy a lower social position in their estimation. There is also evidence to show that those who work in factories and industrial plants in the cities save part of their income to buy land or manage to retain the family property, which may not be giving any dividends but definitely gives them prestige and an assured social status in the village culture (Zaidi, 1959). The respondents of the present study also indicated that, in the village, a person who sells away his inherited property is considered to be unworthy. It is as if he were selling away the bones of his dead forefathers. This is clearly indicative of the villagers' love of land and their attachment to family property.

The basic values important to our respondents, both Hindus and Muslims were: respect for old people both in the family and in the community, respect for one's parents, financial support for one's parents in old age, respect for the religious man, respect of the wife for her husband, and respect for the head of the family. These are the fundamental values on which all the respondents agreed. To them, acting in accordance with these norms is the most important thing in life.

Basically, all six of these values enumerated by the respondents have one virtue in common, namely, respect for age and experience. Older people are respected, not only because they are old, but also because they are supposed to have more knowledge and experience of the world and life. In the same way, the religious man is respected because he knows more about the good things in life and can be their guide for a pious life. The head of the family is the decision-maker because he knows more about what is good for the family. Many of these values have their origin for Muslims in the religious teachings of Islam. One of the sayings of the Prophet is that there is heaven under the feet of your parents. This is the basis of the respect for the parents in their old age. Another rule of conduct for a Muslim is that he must always obey his elders, not only those in the family, but also those who are his neighbors and live in his community. This attitude has, no doubt, been reinforced by the close relationship and interdependence among the villagers. There is a greater sense of security and identification with each other because of communal feelings and also because they have lived together through danger, calamity, and external threats. A long history of isolation of the village may also have added to the feeling of closeness and the attitude of mutual dependence.

Religion has played a great part in guiding the life of the villagers. They have to depend on the *maulvi* for their knowledge of religious practices. The *maulvi* is, therefore, respected as a man of God and as one who is their guide and mentor all the year round. The *maulvi* has, during the course of close associations with various families in the village, emerged as one of the accredited leaders of the village. Many of them coming originally from other places have taken residence in the village, and have now become a part of the village community. But since they still carry on their religious duties, they remain respected and revered.

In addition to the six basic values on which there is 100 per cent agreement among the respondents, both Hindus and Muslims, there are some others which are reported as important by a majority of the respondents. Ninety-two per cent of the Muslims in the two villages think that giving alms to beggars is important. Among the Hindu respondents, only 67 per cent think it important. However, it is generally accepted among Muslims and Hindus that one should not turn away a beggar from his house without alms. For Muslims, this attitude is a part of their belief that one must take out one-fortieth part of his annual income for the poor. This belief is theologically known as *zakat,* which is a duty of every solvent Muslim. Among Hindus also it has been a largely prevalent custom to

feed *sadhu*s and *faqeer*s, for they are the men of God and should
be looked after.

Looking after one's family is both a religious and a social
obligation, and is important everywhere in the world. For our
respondents, both Muslims and Hindus, it is one of the very
important functions of the head of a family. Since the family
in these parts is generally joint, or extended, it becomes a big
burden for the breadwinner if his earnings are not very large.
Even under the most dire circumstances, however, no villager
would think of deserting his family. Ninety-six per cent among
the Muslims and 69 per cent among the Hindus agree that
looking after one's family is important.

Hospitality is another virtue that is part of a villager's
life. In terms of responses, 97 per cent of the Muslims and 78
per cent of the Hindus believed it to be important. However,
it seemed to be of greater importance to Muslims than to
Hindus. Hospitality also is one of the virtues enjoined by Islam.
Traditionally, according to the Prophet, one should share
his meal with his neighbor if he finds that his neighbor has
nothing to eat. The Muslim villagers have extended this virtue
to all guests and outsiders.

There is a difference between Hindus and Muslims also
in attributing importance to the visits to relatives. Apparently
it may not be important to visit a relative, but to maintain
the solidarity of the community and one's own *kunba* group,
it is necessary to keep close and recurrent contacts with one's
kith and kin. This may be one of the reasons why Muslims
everywhere feel for each other as if they are close relatives.
There is historical evidence indicating that Muslims of Pakistan
and India have made great sacrifices for the cause of Muslims of
other countries without caring for the consequences to themselves.

Another less important item but quite significantly discriminating between the attitudes of Hindus and Muslims is
the wearing of a cap on the head. In Muslim homes children
are taught always to cover their head with a cap. In the first
place a cap is needed when one is offering his prayers, and
secondly when meeting elders as a sign of respect. Hence, the

wearing of a cap is supposed to be an indication of one's religious bent of mind. Most of the people in the villages today are found wearing a cap all the time, except when they are sleeping. This is not true of Hindus, who, generally, do not wear a cap. The responses clearly indicate this situation. Among the Muslim respondents, 97 per cent thought it important to wear a cap. Only 5 per cent of the Hindu respondents mentioned its importance.

Just as a "catcher," I had included a supposedly irrelevant item, viz., voting in Union Council elections, in the questionnaire. However, the villagers did not fail to answer it, and their responses indicated that, for a majority of the Muslims, voting is important, although only 38 per cent of the Hindus thought so. One explanation for this lack of interest on the part of the Hindus may be the fact that, because of being in the minority, they do not anticipate one of their men's getting elected in the Union Council. For Muslims, on the other hand, elections may provide a chance "to play politics." There are factions and group loyalties; and the villagers, particularly Muslims, may have much at stake in terms of village politics.

In addition to the value-oriented questions mentioned above, we presented five situations that provided an opportunity for the respondents to evaluate certain types of behavior in terms of traditional value orientation. It has already been pointed out that the villagers still put high value, both economic and social, on landed property. A landless person can never rise in the village social hierarchy. The most respectable position is one in which the person is a hereditary landowner who adds to his land by further purchases. A newly rich person can also join the village social elite, but he will never have the same social position as that of a person who has traditionally been a landowner. However, it is considered shameful if a person is reduced to a position where he has to sell away his landed property. A villager does so only as the last resort. Even so, it is one of the most basic peasant attitudes. This attitude is now in a state of flux because of urbanization and the tendency on the part of the younger generation to migrate to towns for business or for government jobs. Such migrants, of course, do not want to come back to the village and will readily sell away any landed property that they have in the village. The older generation, however, still clings very much to the land, and their attitude is one of reverence for, and identification with, the land.

Related to the attitude stated above is the villagers' dislike for, and resentment of, persons who display their wealth unnecessarily. An unnecessary display of any virtue is considered bad in our culture, but the display of wealth is always considered in bad taste, and only a person with no traditions of family and culture would do such a disgraceful thing. Such display by a person with long social standing in the village, while not approved, is tolerated. But for the person without a traditional family status who shows off his wealth in an attempt to gain status in the village, there is no such tolerance, and he will be considered an upstart who is violating the traditional status hierarchy in order that he gain social status in the village. He may also initiate other changes and may even succeed with the young and uninitiated because of his wealth. Therefore, a person wishing to be admitted into the traditional village social status system must go very slowly, indicating by his behavior that he respects the village social code, particularly by showing respect for the established high families of the village.

It was assumed that, like the person who unnecessarily displays his wealth, the person who tries to impose his leadership over the villagers would also be disliked. However, the results of the study indicated that such was not the case. One reason for this situation may be that in the former case, the person displaying wealth was considered an outsider to the village social hierarchy who was trying to enter it, not through traditional family background, but through something that he may lose at any time. In the case of the person attempting to become a village leader, it is accepted that he belongs to the circle of village "respectables" and, therefore, has a right to assert himself. Another reason may be that such a person is not trying to disturb the established equilibrium of authority, and the imposition of his leadership may only affect a few on the top, who, according to the villagers' conception of authority and leadership, have every right to fight it out among themselves. This vying for power does not disturb the social code of the village. As a matter of fact, it is accepted among the socially high families of the village. To our question, therefore, about what people think of a man who tries to impose his leadership on the village, all the Muslim respondents said that such a person is considered all right, and only 34 per cent of the Hindu respondents said that such a person would be considered bad. This is, however, not a high percentage, and does probably indicate a slightly different thinking of the Hindu respondents for the obvious reason that, among Hindus, the authority pattern is determined by the caste of the leader; and, therefore, anyone who tries to displace the established authority is bad. However, this is only a hypothetical explanation because, even among the Hindus, only one-third considered such a person bad.

The last two questions in regard to basic values related to the villagers' attitude to adultery, both of the husband and of the wife. This is an area of behavior where there can be no disagreement among Muslims and Hindus. We are all aware of the rigidity of peasant morality and the high premium put on male and female morality both before and after marriage, which is the direct result of their respective religious attitudes. It is a sin both for the man and the woman to indulge in adultery, although socially, it is a relatively greater crime for the woman. The male adulterer may, in due course, be forgiven for his misdemeanor; but the female adulteress is never forgiven. Among all the causes of female suicide in our villages, the most frequent is an inability to face a charge of adultery.

It should now be evident from the analysis of the value orientation and social norms of the villagers given above that there is no fundamental difference between Muslims and Hindus in their basic approach and attitudes to life. Though the present discussion was, by necessity, confined to the data collected from the two villages, it is safe, I think, to generalize that the same cultural values are held basic throughout the villages of East Pakistan. And for Muslim villagers, the ethical aspects of these values are also derived from their religious orientation, which is the basis of their attitude to life, morals, and manners, and which means that they share in their own way the values and beliefs of the Muslims in towns and cities.

# CHAPTER VIII

# THE VILLAGE AND THE OUTSIDE WORLD

THE VILLAGES in the Pak-Indian subcontinent have been the focus of attention for a long time. Opinions, therefore, have differed in regard to the reality of the village social organization. About one century ago, Metcalf found villages to be "little republics," which, to him, seemed isolated and self-sufficient. The work of American anthropologists in Indian villages has led them to assume that "the territorial factor, the relation to the soil is not, in India as a whole one of the primary factors in social organization. It is a secondary factor in relation to the two fundamental factors of kinship and caste" (Dumont and Pocock, 1957). There is, however, a third and more balanced perspective, analyses in terms of which have suggested that the village does have a "sociological reality" and, therefore, is a legitimate unit of social organization in the study of the rural society (Orenstein, 1965).

Since the basis of the conclusions about the Indian villages not having sociological reality was the strong caste and kinship ties which, in the case of Hindus, spread beyond the territorial limits of the village, the assumption may have had some justification in relation to Hindu villages. The absence of the institutionalized caste system among Muslims, however, sets the East Pakistan villages apart from the general category of Indian villages. It may, therefore, be noted that the East Pakistan villages have both a sociological and a political reality. These are social units that are, in many ways, self-contained.

This statement, however, does not mean that the villages in East Pakistan are isolated to the point of having no intervillage relationships. As a matter of fact, in spite of their social solidarity the villages have always had social relations with the neighboring villages. As has been discussed earlier, there are the weekly *haat*s, the annual *meelad*s, and visits to shrines and holy men—not to mention times of flood, drought, or disease— that furnish occasions for intervillage contact.

Word of mouth has also and very often served as the source of information and contact for the unlettered villagers of East Pakistan, mostly through the village teacher, the *imam* of the mosque, and the other few people who have contact with the towns. In recent years, of course, such contacts with the outside world have increased manifold. The sources, too, have multiplied in that now certain villages have a few literate people who subscribe to newspapers or may even have a transistor radio. The various attempts of the government to improve the village situation in terms of community develop- ment programs and village modernization schemes have brought them into contact not only with townspeople but even with people from other countries. The villagers in our sample have had this advantage more than most other East Pakistan villagers. In the first place, these villages are only two to three miles away from a semiurban town and are located not far from a cement road. Secondly, since the establishment of a Village Development institution, their contacts with govern- ment and semigovernment agencies have increased many times. Thirdly, a number of American advisors and political leaders have since visited these villages. Besides, the increase in the number of school- and college-going children has also brought the villages nearer the town and the country at large.

An indication of their contact with the outside world may be the possession of modern amenities by the villagers. As stated earlier, our survey indicated that seventeen families in Alipur and fourteen in Ramnagar have their own bicycles; also, six families in Alipur and three in Ramnagar have wrist- watches, out of which one family has two and another has four in the house. One family has a timepiece, and one has a wall clock. One family in Alipur has a gramophone with sixteen records. Eighty families in the two villages have from one to five fountain pens.

Nevertheless, the villagers, especially those above fifty years of age, are still generally ignorant and apathetic to the outside world. Many of them have never gone out of the village; of those who have, only a few have travelled by railway train, and none of them has had the occasion to go near an airplane. Their responses indicated that they are still not very eager to travel, and would prefer to remain in the village. They have no faith in the stranger in towns, and prefer the warm closeness of their fellow villagers. Therefore, they generally learn about new things and events through those few people who, in every village, have traditionally been the town-goers.

However, in view of the postwar emphasis on social change and modernization of villages in developing countries, communication with the outside world through various personal and impersonal channels has assumed greater and deeper significance for social scientists and policy planners alike. We should now be certain about how to communicate most effectively with the isolated villagers.

Surprisingly enough, in spite of a number of village studies in India during the last three or four decades, there has not been much systematic attempt to study the pattern of village communication. There are only some stray discussions of the institutional communication channels and decision-making procedures at the informal or formal village councils or other social occasions in most of the village studies. None of these investigators, however, has gone about it in a systematic way and explored the dynamics of personal and impersonal channels of communication through which, supposedly, the villagers receive most of their information about things relevant to them.

It is assumed that the villagers lean heavily on personal communication for most of their knowledge about things happening outside the village. This is partly owing to illiteracy and partly owing to the fact that villages do not yet have the benefit of the mass media of communication to developing countries. Hence, the significance of personal communication for them.

A number of studies of personal influence have been conducted in the United States (Lazarsfeld, 1960; Mayone, 1952) focussing attention on the pattern of personal influence and communication in different communities. The significance of personal influence in decision-making has also been examined in communities outside the United States. The famous study of Lerner about the transition in the society of the Middle East indicates the presence of the young mobile villagers who carry the news from the outside world to the villages. They are shaping up to be the new-opinion leaders whose prestige and influence rest on their contacts with the outside world through mass communication media and through contact with the towns (Lerner, 1958). Rural sociologists have also brought out the significance of personal communication in their recent studies where they find that, in most rural communities, farmers depend on personal information and advice from others in making their decisions (Rogers, 1962).

Recently the Pakistan Academy for Rural Development, at Comilla, initiated a series of studies relating to diffusion and adoption processes and the pattern of communication and personal influences in the villages in East Pakistan. This effort is the first systematic attempt to focus on the significant area of rural communication patterns. These investigations were designed with a view to "examine the relevance and applicability of the findings of earlier investigations in a village society with a subsistence agricultural economy, high illiteracy, Muslim religion, newly-emerged from British colonial rule and exposed to programmes of community or rural development." In two brief monographs, Rahim (1961; 1965) has attempted to analyze in a systematic manner the pattern of interpersonal influence in diffusion and adoption of agricultural practices, as well as the pattern of personal influence in everyday interpersonal communications among the villagers in East Pakistan. Since the locale of the present study is the same as that in the studies of Rahim, I shall use his results as supplementary to my own, primarily because communication with the outside world was only a part of my general village survey.

I have noted that mass communication media, or what

is generally termed as impersonal channels, are absent from the villages. There are no radios and no one subscribes to a newspaper. Some people may read a newspaper when they visit the town. By and large communication among the villagers takes place through personal contact. Small talk in informal meetings and on social occasions is the predominant channel of communication. There are also those few prominent people in the village to whom people go for advice and for the news of the outside world. These people, according to Rahim's findings, are invariably the friends or the better and "enlightened" farmers in the village. Friendship and success as a farmer are the two main factors in influencing the selection of advisors in the villages. The general nature of such advice relates necessarily to the immediate problems of the villager, namely, agriculture, fertilizers, and other related requirements. The general characteristics of these village advisors, as noted by Rahim, are, "relatively younger in age, larger landholding, frequent contact with the sources of information and early adopters of improved practices." Another interesting conclusion was that formal leadership did not necessarily provide leadership in agriculture. The best village farmer was not generally the elected Basic Democrat of the village.

Rahim also noted in his study that the vertical flow of influence was the most prominent. Influence flowing from persons belonging to higher levels to persons belonging to lower levels was the most common pattern of the flow of influence. The horizontal flow of influence was less prominent. The flow of influence between persons at the same level was frequent and, therefore, an important pattern. It was, however, observed only in the higher levels. The flow of influence from lower to the higher levels was present only in a small number of cases. The flow of influence to the village from outside was also identified as an important pattern. This influence was generally and significantly related to information of a general kind, e.g., current affairs. In general the outside influence percolated down to the village through the top "influentials" of the village (Rahim, 1965).

The role of these men of influence is significant in the

village communication pattern because it has evolved out of a historical necessity. An ordinary person in a village, even today, remains isolated, helpless, and ignorant of the outside world; and, therefore, is obliged, out of necessity, to depend on those who make it their business to keep themselves informed of events and services originating in towns, cities, and government offices. Government officers and town businessmen also find it useful to work with the contact persons who can communicate well with the villagers. The role of the contact persons or the "village influentials" has become essential during the transition from the traditional social organization to a substitute in the village. It has, however, not yet evolved in any functionally effective sense.

The results of Rahim's study discussed and quoted above indicate the general pattern of communication among villager farmers. But since the primary aim of that study was to collect information about agriculture and the diffusion of new practices, the results give only a partial picture of the villagers' contact with the outside world.

The focus of my study in relation to the pattern of communication is the sources and nature of the general information about the world outside the village. An effort was made to find out what things the villagers are interested in, and who or which source brings them such information. A general question asked of them was to identify the "things about which you try to keep yourself informed." Many of them either did not know their own mind or could not verbalize their ideas. Over one-third of them stated that they were not interested in and did not try to keep themselves informed about anything in particular. Those who did try to be informed indicated a wide range of interests, from floods on the land to rockets on the moon. Muslim respondents were more specific than Hindus, and listed their interest in agriculture, floods, peoples' attitude to each other, religion, the cold war, and the business situation outside the village. These responses appear to support my general impression that villagers in East Pakistan are usually more interested about the outside world than are their counterparts elsewhere in Pakistan.

The sources of the villagers' information were "other people," possibly similar to Rahim's "influentials." Some respondents also mentioned the radio and newspapers. These would be the people who are better informed and serve as the villagers' contacts with the town and official agencies.

In the light of my personal observation that the ordinary villager tends to be vague and general in his responses, special care was taken to make the questions elicit concrete aspects of information. I, therefore, asked what they knew about happenings in other parts of East Pakistan. To this question the reply indicated that all of them were interested in what is happening in other parts of the province. The source of their information in this case also was "other people" for 85 per cent of the Muslim respondents. Among the Hindus, however, there were many who mentioned the newspaper as a source. In the case of Hindus, it may be mentioned that they have lost their primary source of information, since most of their relatives have gone over to India since Independence. One or two respondents also mentioned the radio as a source of their information about East Pakistan. The radio news came to them in a shop in the neighboring town.

Continuing my probe about the villagers' interest in the entire country, I inquired if they were interested to know and, if so, what was their source of information about the other wing of the country, i.e., West Pakistan. Thirty-five per cent of the Hindus and 33 per cent of the Muslims indicated little interest in what is happening there. The rest of the respondents said that they try to find out the news about West Pakistan through the newspaper and through people who know.

There seems to be a very clear distinction between Hindus and Muslims in regard to their respective sources of information. For the Hindu respondents generally, the primary source of all general information about the outside world is newspapers. They, therefore, do not depend as much on "other people" for their information. For the Muslims, on the other hand, the primary source seems to be friends, relatives, and casual visitors. These responses constitute a significant division between Muslims and Hindus. The Hindus' reliance on newspapers may also be related to the presence of more educated persons among the Hindus of the villages under study.

I expected that some of the villagers of East Pakistan would also be interested in countries other than their own and India. However, 83 per cent of the Muslims and 71 per cent of the Hindus were not concerned about other countries. Those few who indicated interest in other countries mentioned the United States, the United Kingdom, Japan, China, the Soviet Union, and Germany, about which they try to keep themselves informed. Their source of information about these countries is mostly newspaper reports given them by "other people" who read.

Since it was obvious that the villagers depend on "other people" for information, I attempted to find out the qualification of those who are most frequently approached for information about the outside world. In Rahim's study certain central persons were identified to whom the villagers go for advice, especially about new agricultural practices. But because my questions related to information about local, national, and international affairs, it was expected that a slightly different type of person would be consulted, in that those who know about new methods of agriculture and paddy cultivation may not necessarily know what is happening in East or West Pakistan, or in China, Japan, and the United States.

Response again confirmed my earlier idea that the Hindu respondents consider personal sources unreliable. They do not consider anyone to be well informed in the village. To them, one who reads newspapers could be considered well informed about the outside world. Muslim respondents, on the other hand, considered some village people to be well informed. When asked why, they replied, "because he is educated and because he reads the newspaper." Such a person's sources of information are based on "books, magazines, newspapers, radio, and contact with the town."

It appears from their responses that, for general information, the villagers go to persons who are financially solvent, and thereby acquire a more than average credulity and credit for general information in the eyes of the ordinary villager, who credits such a person with high-level contacts with people in the town. Such is the communication pattern of the village.

Allied with the villagers' pattern of communication with the outside world is their concept of modernization and all that is associated with recent social change. Modernization plans of the various development schemes and the consequent social changes have focussed attention on the attitudes of traditional rural cultures in recent years. The problem assumes great proportions in view of the villagers' faith in the old techniques of adjustment and their glorification of the past.

Unlike industrialized nations where the future represents the hopes and aspiration of the people, in traditional societies the past serves as an anchor to the poor and the old; it becomes a symbol of one's youth to which he clings with fond memories. The present is never very satisfactory in a personal sense. Objectively, things may have changed for the better; but general socioeconomic amelioration is ignored, and personal miseries are exaggerated.

In East Pakistan also the villagers glorify the past in the same vein as the peasants might do in other developing countries. In addition to the survey relating to modernization, forty-five heads of families in the two villages were interviewed to learn especially about their feelings regarding the past and the present and whether they perceived any change in the village during the past twenty years. They were also asked to evaluate the present in the light of their experiences.

The interviewees, as one person, lamented over present miseries and gave a glorified image of the past. Their perception of the present in relation to the past is relevant for a better understanding of the social changes presently in action, although, objectively, the glories of the past may be a mere illusion. Moreover, evidence shows that some of their complaints about the present and many of their illusions of the past are far from the truth. But because dynamic factors of perception are significant variables in the study of social behavior in spite of their lack of correlation with objective facts, some excerpts from the interview, representing their picture of the village as they saw it as a child, are given below:

> In my boyhood, the condition of our village was very good.
> Rice was sold at two rupees a *maund*. One *sari* and one *dhoti* were
> available for one rupee only. There was no scarcity of cattle.
> The villagers were honest. There was no party faction. The ponds
> were full of fish; the cowshed, full of cattle; and the gardens, full of
> fruits. Milk was available in plenty. The villagers were not educated
> (as they are now), but we lived in peace. In those days there were
> not many court cases. The people were happy. We now pine for
> our lost village beauty and tranquility.
>
> At present there is nothing that I saw in my boyhood. The
> government taxes were low. We did not suffer from many wants.
> There were not so frequent natural calamities and there were no
> thefts in the village. We could do what we wanted. At present a
> brother is fighting against brother, and thus destroying each other.

In contrast to that past glory, the present is painted as follows:

> The price of rice is high. We have no cattle in the shed and no
> fruits in the garden. There are no fishes in the pond and no rice
> in the house. The land does not yield as much; it has lost its fertility.
> Milk is scarce. We have no avenue to earn more. The population
> has increased, and men are out of jobs. There is no honesty. There
> is more education and better roads, but no peace. Life has become
> impossible and there is no joy of living. Petty quarrels end in
> bloodshed and prolonged court cases these days.

Obviously, the basic changes felt by the villagers are
primarily economic and social. And these changes, because
they affect the heart of the matter, also affect the harmony
and peace of their social existence. In response to a question
regarding observable changes during the last twenty years,
there is a nostalgic repetition of the scarcity of food and clothing.
One more excerpt may not be out of place.

> The village is over-populated. There is a constant want of
> food. There is no sanitation in the village. The villagers are litigating
> and dishonest. The miseries of the villagers are increased. The
> people do not keep faith in God. The men are trying to fight against
> Nature. No advancement of the country is visible. Thieves and
> swindlers have increased.

Since the majority of our villagers have been living with below-subsistence incomes, any perceptible change would have to show considerable improvement in their living conditions. And because little improvement has been made, "fringe" benefits, like roads and canals, are not impressive to the villagers.

It may be mentioned again at this point that one of the assumptions of this study is that the present East Pakistan society is in a state of transition and, therefore, responses of the villagers should be interpreted in terms of the reactions of a group under stress (Wallace, 1964; Leighton, 1963). Their reactions to various socioeconomic changes are conditioned by the personal experiences of poverty and misery. The contrasting effect in the case of our sample is sharpened because of the great expectations from Independence put into their heads by politicians during the struggle for freedom.

The most urgent and immediate problem for governments in developing countries, therefore, is how to bring about a change of attitude from one of living in the past to hope and confidence in the present and the future. And as has been stated throughout this study, villagers are despondent, apathetic, and even resistant to any change that would, more than likely, upset their routine of life.

Resistance to change in itself is not unusual. One must recognize that resistance to change is a psychological reality, and nowhere do people immediately accept change involving the risk of the unknown. A simple example from East Pakistan villages may explain why people hesitate to accept change, even if it is obviously for their benefit. Let us take the case of accepting improved agricultural practices. An average village farmer in East Pakistan has a small landholding (about 1.7 acres) which, though not enough, at least provides him with subsistence. If he were to experiment with a new method of cultivation he would, from his point of view, run the risk of a poorer yield or possibly no yield at all. He does not have enough land to risk even a small part of it for experimentation. Thus he hesitates to apply a new fertilizer or line-sowing technique of paddy cultivation that, for him, has unknown properties or consequences. It is, therefore, the farmer's perception of an improved technique that is the most important part of all development efforts.

Notwithstanding the psychological resistance to social change, it is a mistake to assume that the people in the villages are satisfied with their present situation, as is often claimed by half-baked urbanites in some of the developing countries. The villagers may be tradition-oriented, fatalistic, and apparently indifferent to change; but they desire change all the same. In these days of frequent contact with the outside world and the varieties of mass communication media, the villagers, in spite of their backwardness and ignorance, have become painfully aware of the differences between their life situation and those of the people in the towns and cities. Village life during the last few decades has become more precarious, which seems to have shaken their apathy and indifference.

The greatest benefit that seems to have accrued from the various attempts of community development, agricultural improvement, and adult education in East Pakistan is the realization on the part of the villagers that their fortunes could be improved. A few decades ago they would probably have only smiled helplessly at any mention of improvement in their situation, whereas it is clear now that they feel that there may be some possibility of a better life for them. Above all, because of their new awareness of the difference between their life and the lives of others, they seem to want a better life.

In the last two chapters the villagers' view of life and their general orientation to the basic values of their society were presented. The attitudes should be considered the general sociocultural background within which villagers in East Pakistan have been brought up. The present village culture may more profitably be conceptualized as facing the change from the traditional agrarian culture, with its associated value system, to modernization, with its industrial-technological complex of values and attitudes. This change has caused what may be characterized as sociocultural disorganization. During this phase of the transition there is a tendency for a person to cling to the old while being aware of the pull of the new (Wallace, 1964). The villager in East Pakistan is very much confused and indecisive about the new changes, but evidently he is very much attracted to them.

As a consequence of the desire for change there seems to have occurred some relaxation of the traditional fatalism in the sense that, as was mentioned above, not only is there a desire for change but also a certain feeling that the change is possible. This positive attitude is true of both Muslim and Hindu respondents in our two villages. There is, however, still a bigger group which feels that it may not be possible, under present circumstances, to change many aspects of village life. Further probing revealed that, though change is considered possible, it can only be brought about through the efforts and help of the government. This is the same attitude of dependence towards the government and lack of faith in one's own efforts that has long persisted among villagers. A few respondents— 10 per cent of the Muslims and 3 per cent of the Hindus—also leave the matter to the will of God. This incongruity between the positive attitude to change and the simultaneous lack of faith in one's capability to bring it about is a characteristic feature of behavior during a transitional phase in society. Most of the responses of our villagers are typical of such behavioral indecision accompanied by positive attitudes.

Two other questions were included in the survey to find out what modern amenities the respondents would like to have in their village and in their house. From the list of items provided by them, one gets the impression that, given a choice, they would like to transform the entire village, including their own house, into a modern locality in a modern country.

For the village, they wanted electricity, roads, big shops, a cinema, a college, a hospital, tube wells, a bank, civil and criminal courts, a good market, cars, and buses; for the house, they wanted electricity, a radio, that their house be made of brick, a tube well, a sanitary latrine, china crockery, a gramophone, a telephone, a sewing machine, and some good furniture. The list would have been longer still if the villagers had seen other things; but since most of the respondents have not travelled beyond the nearby town of Comilla, it is necessarily limited to the objects they have seen there.

Since the focus of this study is the dynamics of perceptions rather than merely a listing of modern amenities for the home and the community, I tried to uncover the villagers' stereotypes of a modern man and woman. The respondents' total cognition of social change and modernization is likely to be determined by what they perceive to be "modern." To the villagers a modern man is essentially an educated man with a college background and a facility of communication with urban people. They also emphasize the difference between themselves and a modern man by indicating that the modern man reads the newspaper and knows what is happening everywhere. About one-third of the Hindu respondents also felt that one is modern because "he is not like us," which is what is meant by "sharpening the difference" between rural and urban life.

I noticed that not only do the respondents realize the advantages of being modern but also wish that such a person belonged to their own family. Thirty-five per cent of the Hindus and 70 per cent of the Muslims said that they would like their own son to be modern. The rest of them did not know their own mind, which supposedly may mean that in view of their present circumstances they could not visualize their son's going to college. There is possibly a greater sense of helplessness in the "do not know" type of response in this context.

Again the East Pakistan village society is predominantly a male society. Women stay indoors, and generally have no social life. They may gossip and quarrel among themselves, but apart from that their life is a long drudgery from morning till evening. The villager's idea of a good woman has already been discussed. This same conception determines his attitude to the modern woman. The village people are generally not happy with the role of a woman in a modern society. This attitude is the conservative in them. Village women themselves may tend to agree with their men folk in this respect, possibly because, to them, the contrast of their life with that of a city-bred, college-educated modern woman is not yet sharply in focus. They are not yet aware of the difference that moderniza-tion could make to their life.

As regards the characteristics of a modern woman as seen by the respondents, a majority of them either do not respond or are not sure what to say. Their difficulty is under-standable because many of them have not had much chance to observe a modern woman at close quarters. Also, they may have had certain reservations against saying what they really feel. However, from the few responses that were made, we get the picture of a modern woman as one who is educated but has no feminine grace and dignity, no hesitation in com-municating with strange men, and no scruples or modesty. It is clear, though, that the emphasis, even in these few responses, is on being educated. The other "virtues" are painted as a result of the normal stereotype of an educated woman. How-ever, it may be suggested that a college education is generally a symbol of modernity for the average village men and women. Education for children, therefore, is ardently desired by the parents in the village.

This then is how the East Pakistani villagers look at moderni-zation schemes that are aimed at bringing about a general social change in their lives. One can clearly discern contradic-tions between attitudes and behavior. There is also indecision and reticence about many aspects of change. The various responses to the questionnaire generally make out the present villagers of East Pakistan to be quite progressive and yet conservative in many of their stereotypes and prejudices. They are quite progressive when it comes to desiring the modern amenities of life, be it education for the children or owning a sewing machine. They would not like to walk to the town if they could catch a bus or get a lift in a car. They would also like to possess all good things that make life modern and worth living. In this sense they are as mundane in their attitudes as their counterparts in any modern industrial society. Indecision and conflict may occur when they are faced with a choice between the established social and cultural values and way of life on the one hand and the modern, industrial-oriented approach to life on the other.

They would resist all attempts to bring their women out of *pardah,* and they would castigate any person violating the moral and social norms of the community. They may, however, accept a new variety of fertilizer or a new method of cultivation and irrigation; but they would also stick to many of their prejudices and superstitions. And this partaking of both worlds does not appear contradictory to them, neither does it seem to affect, in any way, their way of life and its value orientation. Because the radio and electricity make life easier without interfering with their fundamental beliefs, they are both welcome and desirable.

# CHAPTER IX

# THE VILLAGE CULTURE UNDER STRESS

THERE ARE two major concepts to be considered in a discussion of village culture under stress. The first is the term "village culture", which represents ideas, belief systems, values, and the norms of behavior regulating the life of a community— the nonmaterial features of life. The second concept has to do with the term "stress", which is defined as "any influence, whether it arises from the internal environment or from the external environment, which interferes with the satisfaction of basic needs or which disturbs or threatens to disturb the stable equilibrium" (Engel, 1953).

When, therefore, the reference to the village culture being under stress is made, it is assumed that certain influences, mainly from the external environment, are either disturbing or threatening to disturb the stable equilibrium of life in the villages of East Pakistan. Specifically, the reference is to the various external influences attempting to modernize the villages. These two concepts of village culture and stress, therefore, imply our two major assumptions about the East Pakistan village society:

First, that the village culture of East Pakistan is easily distinguishable from that of West Pakistan. In West Pakistan there are still fairly big landholders in the villages. There are none in East Pakistan since the *zamindari* system was abolished by the East Pakistan government soon after Independence, in 1947. Even before this period, the *zamindars* were mostly all Hindus and there was no great social and economic difference among the Muslim villagers. Today, the difference is still less.

A majority of the East Pakistani villagers belong to the lower or lower-middle class economically. In West Pakistan, on the other hand, there is a distinct, though small, class of land-holders who are economically, educationally, and socially better off than the rest of the villagers. Besides, there is no steep social hierarchy in East Pakistan like that in West Pakistan, where the general social classification in villages is categorized in terms of landed aristocracy and the poor peasantry (Honigmann, 1958).

Second, the premise that the village culture, a major sector of Pakistan society, is under stress from a variety of socioeconomic changes being introduced in the country. The reasons and the basis for this assumption have been analyzed in an earlier paper (Zaidi, 1964). Suffice it to say here that the sociocultural situation in the different parts of the country clearly indicates signs and symptoms of social disorganization. It is obvious from the general sense of disillusionment and frustration in the country that the society is still in a state of flux. In a scale of transition we can locate the present Pakistan society as being in transition from the stage of disorganization to that of reorganization, during which, it has been noted, a society goes through the conflict between clinging to the old ways and longing to accept the new. This conflict may give rise to a number of ideologies, policies, and anchorage points. The group attempts to make compromises and may often arrive at some meaningful solution of its problems and dilemmas (Wallace, 1961).

A number of specific patterns of change have been known to occur in societies subjected to similar stresses. For example, one is the almost axiomatic statement that there occurs a change from the extended family to the nuclear family which, in turn, modifies the interrelationship and the pattern of authority within the family. Such a change would involve numerous adjustment difficulties for old men, women, and children. It may also generate incompatibility of the traditional role differentiation leading even to incompatibility of the traditional value system and beliefs. It is also likely to involve the solidarity of traditional family affiliations.

In almost all the developing countries loyalty to family is of the greatest consequence. Any dislocation of established family relationships is tantamount to a cultural revolution. The casual and almost indifferent attitude of a modern industrial society toward family, is nothing short of a social and cultural crime in traditional societies. Once this anchor is gone or weakened, the consequences may be disastrous in terms of generating forms of psychosocial pathology in the society.

It is in terms of this conceptual framework that the social and technological plans of rural development are assumed to act as situations of stress for the village culture.

Many of the features of the village are being subjected to great stress, both physical and psychological. Attempts are being made to modernize village life in terms of new health measures, improved agricultural practices, the use of power pumps and tractors, better roads, and better physical facilities. These changes in traditional village life would necessitate social-psychological changes in terms of new adjustment techniques on the part of tradition-oriented villagers. These changes may, therefore, be conceived of as the sources of stress on the village culture. Village people love their old ways and naturally resist the adoption of new practices. They are facing a conflict between wanting to keep to the old ways and, at the same time, desiring the benefits of modern life. This conflict contributes to the stress on the villagers.

Historically, the first official plan of village development was initiated in East Pakistan during the 1930's, under a scheme called Rural Reconstruction. The plan had to be abandoned because of a number of administrative snags and bottlenecks. In 1954 the Government of Pakistan launched its first country-wide community development program generally known as V-AID (Village Agricultural and Industrial Development). In 1960, V-AID was replaced by a more comprehensive development program, under the name of Basic Democracy.

In East Pakistan, the Comilla Academy was started in 1959 with the specific aim of training the middle-level officers of the government in the application of social science theories to rural development. Under the dynamic leadership of its able Director, it has now developed into an institution experimenting with new techniques of rural development generally referred to as the Comilla approach (Khan, 1964). The experimental approach of the Academy is broadly based on the principle of training the villagers to develop themselves through building up village cooperative groups.

Besides, the government is also attempting to introduce many-sided plans of industrialization and urbanization in order to develop the country as a whole. Three five-year plans have already been launched, and the entire Pakistan society is being covered under these plans. The ultimate objective is to modernize the society.

These various plans of social and technological change are having their impact on the life of the people. The initial reactions to these are indicative of shocked resistance, followed by sociocultural conflicts (Zaidi, 1966). The people are caught in the midst of certain new developments which are upsetting, or threatening to upset, their stable equilibrium, by discarding the old and familiar ways of life. At the village level the stress is greater because the resistance to change is stronger. Villagers are still poorly prepared for the various readjustments that the society will have to undergo in the process of transition from the old to the new. During the transition the old and familiar adjustive techniques are likely to be rendered inadequate and unsuitable, thus involving the learning of new adjustive devices and know-how.

For example, there must be a transition from a monsoon economy to an irrigation economy. East Pakistan is an area of heavy rainfall where the farmers have always used monsoon water for irrigating their land. There never was much need for storing water for irrigation because the crop pattern followed the monsoon seasons in general. Under the rural development schemes, however, new and more crops per year are being introduced, which means more water needed when there is no monsoon, thus necessitating the storage of water to irrigate the land. Farmers are being persuaded and educated to irrigate the land and get more crops, thereby introducing both a change in the old crop pattern and an emphasis on irrigation for better economic results. This situation constitutes a drastic change in the sense that farmers are persuaded to use power pumps for irrigation and thus enter the mechanized agriculture age in one leap—a transition from the indigenous agriculture to improved cultivation practices.

A transition from a propitiating attitude to the idea of control of nature through knowledge and scientific skill is required. The fatalistic attitude of the villagers towards God, Nature, and the Unseen has already been noted. This attitude is probably characteristic of a pre-scientific and pre-industrial approach to natural phenomena. Villagers are now being taught that they can change their life situation with the help of scientific devices. They are being persuaded to practice new, improved methods of agriculture, health, sanitation, and animal husbandry. Through the adult education booklets, by agricultural demonstrations, and with the use of insecticides and scientific medicine, they are being given their first taste of science and its blessings. They are also being taught not to be fatalistic and wait for things to happen. Such a change would mean a complete transformation of their approach to life, health, and disease. The results are still not visible. There is resistance, indifference, and the shrugging of shoulders; but the impact of these changes would not take very long to show. The transition from the unscientific and fatalistic approach to the scientific and the rational, though difficult, is under way. The final adjustment may follow a period of stressful confusion, indecision, and even disillusionment.

Transition from the joint family system to the nuclear family must also take place. The disintegration of the joint family and the period of transition before the new pattern of the nuclear family takes roots may be the most crucial for the village culture. With younger men going to work in factories and mills, the idea of a nuclear family is already appealing to them because the burden of supporting a large family with an insufficient income is affecting their own living standards.

They prefer an urban life with its freedom from agricultural labor. The breakup of the traditional family is clearly visible in the villages. The result may be a disregard and even violation of the basic community values on the part of the younger boys, and disapproval, irritation, and curses from the older generation (Husain, 1956), which may be only the first sign of the social disorganization resulting from this transition.

A transition from family strength through numbers to family planning is required. One of the criteria of the family strength and even its social position in the traditional village society is the number of its male members, which, in the past, may have determined the family's fighting and earning potential. For the Muslims this attitude towards the number of men in the family has probably come from their ideological affiliations with the Arabs where, for the tribal social structure, it was an important factor. A large family, therefore, was desired. There is some evidence to indicate that this attitude is generally held among Muslim villagers in East Pakistan. Forty-six per cent of our Muslim respondents thought that the number of men in the family determined its social status in the village. The relatively smaller frequency of response may be owing to the recent work in family planning and birth control carried out in the villages. There is, however, no question that a transition in the attitude towards the family is in evidence. There is now less emphasis on polygamy and the number of sons in the family, which may partly be owing to the absence of enough to eat and partly the result of family planning programs. The crucial factor is that day in and day out the villagers are being reminded of the population pressure and the need to give up their old concept of family strength through numbers.

And, finally, a transition from the idea of a leader as an advocate to that of an organizer is necessary. The traditional image of the leader is one of an advisor in difficulties, an advocate for the cause of the community, and a liaison between the village and government agents. Their advocacy in particular consisted of pleading for remission of delay in the payment of land revenue or getting the villagers out of trouble through their own influence. Under the recent change of agricultural practices with emphasis on learning the new techniques of improved agriculture, the village leaders are called upon to assume the organization of literacy classes, cooperative groups, and demonstration teams for the rural development programs. This new role of the village leaders has been excellently demonstrated by the Comilla approach in East Pakistan (Khan, 1964). The transition may be difficult both for the village leaders and the poor farmers because it involves the assumption of a new role and learning of a new problem-solving technique for which none of them is trained or psychologically prepared. The villagers still look upon the *sirdars* and *maatbars* as advocates for their cause. The transition may be ultimately achieved, though right now the stress caused by the adjustment of the social relationships in the village may be disturbing and frustrating.

In light of the above analysis and my earlier discussion of value orientation, I should now like to discuss the conflict of values and the symptoms of social disorganization in the village culture. Since the purpose of the various plans of rural development and technological changes is to bring about modernization in the society, it is pertinent to ponder over the consequences of these attempts on the prevailing sociocultural norms and values. The basic value system of the village culture is unquestionably in contrast to that of modern industrial society. The present value orientation is neither conducive nor appropriate and legitimate for an industrially oriented society. It seems almost inevitable that serious value conflicts would occur and lead to many morbid and pathological consequences.

In the West, industrialization and urbanization followed a natural course of social and legal development. When the change came it was familiar and expected. The change naturally led to the development of institutions appropriate to the process. In the East, on the other hand, people have been caught in the tide. They are so used to their familiar way of life with its characteristic fatalism and dependence on God that, to them, these social changes appear a heresy in many cases.

As Lerner (1958) puts it, "Whereas the traditional man tended to reject innovation by saying 'it has never been thus,' the contemporary Westerner is more likely to ask 'does it work?' and try the new way without further ado."

This contrast between the perception and attitudes of the Westerner and those of traditional people to change puts my earlier discussion in a clearer perspective. Those aspects of the village culture which seem to be most vulnerable to the stress of sociocultural change are:

## Family Relations

In a traditional society the family provides the emotional, social, and even the financial security to its members. In the joint family the resources are pooled, and the head of the family is responsible for meeting all the needs of the men, their wives, and children. No one questions the loyalty of the members to the family name, prestige, and property. Nor does a member ever feel insecure even when unemployed or abandoned by friends. The family is the real emotional anchor for the rich and the poor alike.

This familial pattern cannot survive under the impact of industrialization and the lure of an urban life. The conflict between loyalty to the joint family and the desire to provide for one's own wife and children first has already begun to show in East Pakistan. The following excerpt, from a paper published earlier, about how a rural youth finds working in an industrial organization will illustrate the point:

He faces the initial difficulty of adjusting to a largely urban and industrial environment for which his rural background is entirely unsuited. The stereotypes, beliefs and attitudes appropriate to a rural family pattern make the adjustment to an industrial family pattern very difficult for him. The joint pattern of our large rural families comes into clash with the responsibilities of a new pattern. The worker is naturally inclined to this new pattern, but the affiliations with other members of the family keep him undecided. He mostly wants and tries to retain these affiliations with other relatives in the village, as evidenced by the large number of absences due to "urgent business at home." Thus he is torn between two loyalties. (Zaidi, 1959)

Associated with the adjustment difficulty of living in an industrial setting is the villagers' loyalty to the land and the habitat. As noted earlier, one of the major criteria of a person's or a family's social classification in the village is the size of the landed property. This scale of values is alien to a modern industrial society. Many of our village youth who go out to work in a factory cannot easily get over this sense of social evaluation; many come to work in the factory with the specific objective of earning enough to retain the family property or to buy more of it. They save money while at work even though most often such savings compete with the equally strong desire for a better standard of living. This attempt to maintain "two homes" and the subsequent conflict of loyalty leads both to economic difficulties and to social frustrations affecting their physical and mental well-being.

**Personal versus Community Orientation in Achievement**
In the traditional village culture a socially and financially successful man makes the entire community proud of him. For example, if a village boy or his family settles in a town in connection with his business or profession, any member of his village community while visiting the town makes it almost obligatory on himself to visit and even stay with him. "He is a village fellow" or "he is from my village" is the common expression of pride. The city-dwelling youth and his family would welcome the village guest unless, during their stay in the city, they have been "infected" with the selfish ways of the city life. In a traditional culture one does not show off the fruits of his success, he shares the pride of success with his community. He lets the other members of the village feel that he belongs to them and has achieved success through their blessings. In the changing value orientations, such a role-expectation from a city-dwelling family involved with its new status symbols and personal achievement motivations, with the increasing demands of new and higher achievements, and with the stress of maintaining its new-found social status would generate a variety of conflicts and numerous embarrassing and frustrating situations.

## Social Mobility

An important factor likely to disturb the homeostatic balance of the traditional social hierarchy is the shift in the pattern of social mobility owing to technological and social change. Traditionally, the village society has had a well-defined and relatively permanent system of social stratification in which factors like the size of the landholding and family aristocracy play a major role. Persons born in a certain family have an ascribed status which, in the context of the village social classification, is not normally altered by one's achieved status. The son of a "lower class" family, even though he may attain some worldly success may, on returning to his village home, be expected to behave in the same humble way as his poor father did in the presence of the village elders. This pattern of social relationship is sure to suffer when the criteria of social status change. The old criteria of age, family descent, and landholding have no value or functional utility in an industrial-urban milieu. On the other hand, a readjustment of the traditional social stratification may mean a total breakdown of the social structure and its valued institutional behavior patterns.

## Pattern of Authority and Leadership

In the village families authority rests in the head, who is the oldest member both in age and in relationship. Authority in the village rests with an informal council of elders who have had this prerogative through inheritance and through the normal channels of social classification. There would be no challenge to this authority as long as the traditional cultural pattern is adhered to. But with the new wave of modernization, more education, and variety of government jobs, the pattern of village leadership and authority is undergoing a change. There is evidence to show that, in East Pakistan village society, conflict with and violation of the traditional authority is already beginning to show. Husain (1956), reporting on a survey of factory workers mostly drawn from East Pakistan villages, describes the present situation thus: "Finding parental discipline too irksome, they were enjoying their newly found independence and having a good time in the company of their mates and were not anxious to visit home or share in the family responsibility." This is the present attitude of the semiliterate factory worker towards the village authority. The consequences of a more widespread social change can easily be predicted on the basis of this attitude, even in the early stages of industrialization in Pakistan.

## Position of Women

Another vulnerable point in the village culture is the position of women in a predominantly Muslim Pakistan. Although Islam places men and women on equal footing with appropriate divisions of labor, in practice village women have not been given the status they deserve. They stay at home and toil all day long with only an occasional break for gossip or quarrel to reduce the monotony. The situation, however, is already changing in terms of the male attitude toward female education. Under the new impetus with more universal education and job opportunities for all, the results could be shattering for village life. It would hit the family security; parent-child relationship; rural attitudes and prejudices; and above all, the emotional support which the child enjoys at home because of the mother's staying all day long. Undoubtedly, this change would make women economically self-supporting; but it may also make, as many suspect, the women less "home-minded," and even emotionally insecure in the face of competition for marriage.

At present village girls are secure in the knowledge that their parents or older relatives will find a husband for them. They also enjoy the security of their parental home in case of divorce or the death of their husband. It may probably be correct to say that the present pattern of the village family is far less anxiety-producing for women than the modern homes in industrial societies, although it is also true that this situation does not justify keeping women illiterate and useless for anything except child-bearing and child-rearing.

I have indicated the extent to which the village culture is under stress. The significant spots likely to have the most intense and far-reaching impact of the stress have also been identified. The culture is still in a state of transition, and the process of change is actively in operation. All that can be done with any amount of confidence at this stage is to point out the direction of change and anticipate certain well-known consequences, which I have done throughout this study. To further support these anticipated consequences of social change the following excerpts from an investigation of the human and social impact of technological change in East Pakistan are presented in conclusion (Husain, 1956). They amply illustrate how and in what way a traditionally agrarian culture reacts to technological and social changes:

The single worker coming to the factory finds himself in a strange environment and tastes his freedom from family discipline as well as from the strict code of moral restraint which is prevalent in the villages. . . . There is no doubt that quite a few of the workers fall in evil company and take to drinking and dissipation. The incidence of venereal diseases seems to be high. Cases of unnatural offences were also reported. . . . Religious habits of the workers seem to change with the length of service in the factory. Thus among the factory workers with less than six months of service, only 36 per cent said their daily prayers which is very much below the proportion of workers in all age groups (60.3%) saying their prayers. . . . *Peers*, *Maulana*s and *Maulvi*s (religious guides) have a great hold on the masses in this province (East Pakistan). (But) as one goes through the case studies made, it becomes abundantly clear that while many workers still have faith in them, it is no longer a blind faith. . . . The typical factory worker in East Pakistan is probably on balance, a maladjusted individual. From the present survey it appears that the symptoms of maladjustment are much more numerous and marked in matters like conditions of work and amenities, contact with one's family and the treatment by the supervisor. (pages 193, 196, 203, and 249)

This, then, is the picture of the village culture in East Pakistan as I found it at the time of my investigation. Hopefully, it may serve as a guideline for more intense and sharply focused investigations in the future.

# APPENDIX:
## Household Articles of an Average Village Family

### FURNITURE FOR SITTING OR SLEEPING

*Balish*  A Persian word for a pillow stuffed with cotton or rags.

*Chatai*  A coarse mat of different sizes and sorts.

*Chawki*  A wooden bedstead.

*Chhota chawki*  A wooden stool.

*Dhusa*  A quilt mostly found in well-to-do houses.

*Kantha*  A covering made of old clothes and rags instead of a quilt.

*Mora*  A cane, or bamboo, stool to sit on.

*Pati*  A mat of fine texture.

*Piri*  A plank seat.

### EATING UTENSILS

*Badna*  A brass, or earthen, water pot.

*Basan*  A crockery plate.

*Bati*  A brass cup.

*Ghati*  A brass water pot.

*Glash*  A glass for drinking water, mostly made of brass.

*Hanki,* or *shani*  An earthen plate.

*Khada*  A stone cup.

*Kharti*  An earthen water pot.

*Khora*  An earthen cup.

*Thal*  A plate, generally of brass.

### COOKING UTENSILS

*Baoli*  An iron or brass implement for placing the cooking utensils over the hearth, or for taking them down.

*Bokna,* or *boga*  A brass pot.

*Dailer-kata*  A pestle used for grinding pulses after they are boiled. It is made of both iron and wood.

| | |
|---|---|
| *Deg* | A pot for cooking rice, especially for large groups, made of copper and zinc. |
| *Degehi* | Large and small copper vessels invariably used by Muslims. |
| *Deova,* or *hata* | A wooden ladle. |
| *Jhanjhar* | An earthen perforated vessel for straining water when washing rice. |
| *Kalsi* | A brass, or earthen, water pitcher. |
| *Karai* | An iron pan. |
| *Mala* | A cup made of a cocoanut shell. |
| *Pata,* or *puta* | A flat stone and a stone roller used in grinding condiments for curry. |
| *Patil* | An earthen, or aluminum, pot smaller than a *raing*. |
| *Raing* | An earthen pot. |
| *Shara* | An earthen pot cover. |
| *Tagari* | A bowl. |

### INSTRUMENTS FOR CUTTING OR DIGGING

| | |
|---|---|
| *Bati dao* | A fish knife. |
| *Hat dao* | A large hand knife. |
| *Kanchi* | A sickle. |
| *Khanta* | A digging hoe. |
| *Kodal* | A spade. |
| *Kural* | An axe. |
| *Sarta* | A betel-nut cracker. |

### MISCELLANEOUS IMPLEMENTS

| | |
|---|---|
| *Aina* | A Persian word for mirror. |
| *Baithak* | A *hukka* stand made of wood, earth, or brass. |
| *Bansi* | A fishhook. |
| *Chalain* | A sieve. |
| *Changa* | A bamboo ladder. |
| *Chhati* | A cloth umbrella. |
| *Chhia* | A pestle for *gail*. |
| *Chimta* | A pair of tongs made of iron, or wood. |
| *Dhenki* | A pedal used in husking rice. |
| *Gachha* | An earthen, or wooden, stand for the lamp. |
| *Gamla* | An earthen vessel containing fodder for cattle. |
| *Hain* | A comb made of bamboo. |

| | |
|---|---|
| *Hocha, or pala* | A bamboo trap for catching fish. |
| *Hok* | A piece of hard wood with a pointed end used for making holes in the ground when putting stakes around a field. |
| *Hukka* | A hubble-bubble pipe for smoking tobacco, usually made of cocoanut shell. |
| *Jhata* | A broom. |
| *Jongra* | A tortoise-like covering for the head and shoulders against rain, made of kuruch leaves. |
| *Kail, or gail* | Wooden mortar. |
| *Kalki* | An earthen bowl for tobacco placed on top of the *hukka* when smoking. |
| *Katha* | A basket measure for grain. |
| *Konch* | A fish harpoon. |
| *Kula* | A winnowing basket. |
| *Kupi* | An earthen, or tin, pot to contain kerosine and the lamp wick. |
| *Luri patil* | An earthen pot filled with water and mud, used in giving a fresh coating of mud to the floor of the house every morning. |
| *Patla* | A covering for the head and shoulders against rain, made of leaves. |
| *Phorbash* | A bamboo needle used in thatching houses. |
| *Ser* | A cane measure containing one *seer* (a little over two pounds in weight) |
| *Sik* | An iron rod for cleaning the smoking pipe, or tube. |
| *Sunch, or bar sunch* | A small or large needle. |
| *Tukri* | A basket. |

### RECEPTACLES

| | |
|---|---|
| *Ailla* | An earthen pot for keeping fire. |
| *Chhala* | A sack for carrying, or storing grain. |
| *Dol* | A large, cylindrical basket made of bamboo mats used for storing grain. |
| *Dola* | A small bamboo basket. |
| *Dula* | A small basket for keeping fish. |
| *Jhail* | A small, bamboo-made box used for keeping toilet articles. |
| *Jhaka* | A large bamboo basket. |
| *Kalsi* | A large earthen pot for keeping rice. |

|            |                                                    |
|-----------:|----------------------------------------------------|
| *Macha*     | A bamboo platform for keeping the grain pot.       |
| *Matki*     | An earthen jar.                                    |
| *Petara*    | A bamboo-work box for keeping clothes.             |
| *Saji*      | A small bamboo basket.                             |
| *Sikka*     | A jute net bag for holding earthen pots.           |
| *Sindhuk*   | A small wooden chest found in better houses.       |
| *Tamaku-dibi* | A bamboo vessel for keeping tobacco.             |

# GLOSSARY

*Almirah*   A wardrobe placed against a wall, but not attached to it. It may be made of wood or steel. In the villages, *almirah*s are generally made of wood.

*Aquiqua*   A Muslim religious ceremony celebrating the birth of a child. It is a public occasion, the festivity of which depends upon the financial capability of the family. The essential element of the occasion is to sacrifice one goat upon the birth of a female child, and two goats upon the birth of a male child. Approved by orthodox Islam.

*Azaan*   The procedure of calling the Faithful to the mosque five times a day to join the prayer congregation. The recital is done in Arabic, and begins with "God is great."

*Barat*   The bridal party that starts from the groom's house and stops at the bride's house.

*Bari*   A house, or living quarters. It may also refer to a family, or kinship location.

*Barkat*   Literally, "blessing," and is used to denote a mysterious wonder-working force that is looked upon as a blessing from God, a blessed virtue. A person who possesses *barkat* is a saint. According to orthodox Muslim belief, no man possessed more *barkat* than the Prophet of Islam.

*Basha*   The structure of a house.

*Burqa*   A loose garment used by Muslim women as a veil to cover themselves. It is put over the normal dress, and covers the body from head to foot. It has two netted holes for the eyes. An approved social custom. The Islamic injunction only enjoins upon women to keep away from the company of men.

*Chowdhary*   A landlord. Now generally used as a surname of the families. In certain parts of the country it also means the head of a village, or the head of one of the village groups.

*Chowki*   A hard, wooden bed made with four legs on which planks are nailed to give it a flat surface. In certain parts of the subcontinent, the term also means a location, or headquarters, e.g., *Police chowki*.

*Chowkidar*   An incumbent of a position in the local administration responsible originally for guarding a location. In some parts of Pakistan and India he is made responsible for a number of villages; and his main duties are reporting births, deaths, and crimes to the local administration.

*Dargah*   The resting place of a saint. It may mean the place where a holy man or a saint is living away from the worldly hum and bustle. It may also mean the place housing the grave of a saint where people throng to beg for his blessing.

*Deo-angshi*   A supernatural being capable of harming human beings. It is believed to be residing in ponds. This belief is not approved by *maulvi*s or orthodox Islam.

*Dewan*   It was an office under the Muslim rulers roughly equivalent to a minister in the modern sense.

*Dhoti*   Men's wear in the villages, covering only the lower part of the body from the waist down. It is typically a Hindu dress.

*Eid*   Happiness, or making merry. Among Muslims there are two festive occasions known as *Eid*. The first *Eid*, known as *Eid-ul-Fitr*, falls on the first day following the month of Fasting. It is the first of the tenth month of the Muslim calendar. The second, known as *Eid-ul-Azha*, occurs on the occasion of *Hajj*, the pilgrimage to Mecca, the Muslim holy land in Saudi Arabia, on the tenth day of the last month of the Muslim calendar. It is also known as the *Eid* of sacrifice because, on three continuous days beginning with the day of *Hajj*, it is obligatory on all solvent Muslims to sacrifice something precious to God. A goat, or a cow, or a camel is sacrificed on this occasion. The sacrifice originated with the dream of the Prophet Ibrahim, wherein he was asked by God to sacrifice his son Ismail. Ibrahim yielded to the command, but before the son could be sacrificed, he was replaced by a lamb.

*Fard*   Literally, an "estimate," or "record." This is the paper on which the gifts to be exchanged in marriage are listed.

*Faqeer*   A mendicant. Originally it meant one who has renounced his desire for worldly goods and lives happily in poverty. The word is now misused for beggars.

*Gita*   A Hindu hold book believed to contain the sayings and doings of Lord Krishna, a Hindu god.

*Haat*   A village market place.

*Haji*   One who has performed his pilgrimage to Mecca, *Hajj*.

*Hajj*   Pilgrimage to Mecca.

*Hajjam*   A barber. He is the professional circumcisor in the villages.

*Hakim*   Literally, "a wise man," or "a philosopher." A practitioner of the *Unani* (Greek) system of medicine, refined by the Muslims.

*Imam*   Literally, "a leader." A person who leads the congregation in the mosque.

*Jarigan*   A kind of folk song that the villagers enjoy singing in a chorus or group.

*Jatra*   A kind of folk opera, a musical drama of a historical type.

*Jihad*   Literally, "to make efforts." This is one of the five pillars of Islamic faith enjoining on all Muslims to crusade against evil. There are three degrees of *Jihad:* (i) simply to condemn an evil in one's heart and to oneself, (ii) to announce by word of mouth that one condemns the evil, and (iii) to take up arms to fight the evil. Historically, *Jihad* has come to mean the holy wars fought by Muslims against non-Muslims in the cause of Islam.

*Jinn*   Equivalent to English *geni*. Muslims believe that *jinns*, individual beings, are one of the many creations of God. They are believed to be both good and bad, as are human beings. The bad ones harrass humans if offended in any way.

*Kaába*   The place in Medina, Saudi Arabia, towards which Muslims face while praying. *Hajj* is performed in Kaába.

*Kabiraj*   A practitioner of the pseudoscientific system of Ayurvedic medicine quite popular among the poor Hindus.

*Kani*   A measure of land equal to four-tenths of an acre.

*Keertan*   Devotional Hindu songs in praise of the gods.

*Khal*   A place inhabited by a supernatural being.

*Khankah*   A place where a holy man or a saint lives and prays in seclusion. During the Muslim rule in India, *khankah* was an important institution of religious learning and piety. The Muslim mystics mostly lived in *khankah,* which was looked upon by Muslims as sacred.

*Kunba*   A family or kinship group generally comprising the descendents of one person.

*Maatbar*   Literally, "the reliable." In the East Pakistan village social structure, the *maatbar* is generally one of the prominent persons of the village, and is a member of the informal village council.

*Madrasah*   A place where lessons are given. It is a school with Islamic religious orientation. *Madrasah* has its own system of education and evaluation.

*Majumdar*   A family surname in East Pakistan for both Hindus and Muslims. Originally, it meant a family with landed property.

*Maulvi*   An Arabic word meaning "pertaining to God." It has a generic connotation referring to anyone who, in appearance or in truth, is a religious man. It is a class of *madrasah*-educated persons who devote their lives to religious pursuits on a very meager income under the present-day secular English education system. A really educated *maulvi* is well versed in Islamic religious learning.

*Maund*   A measure of weight equal to eighty-two pounds. Its units are *seer*s. One *maund* is equal to forty *seers*, and a *seer* is, therefore, about two pounds in weight.

*Meelad*   Its full title is *Meelad-un-Nabi*, which literally means "birth of the Prophet of Islam." It is a gathering of Muslims in which the details of the Prophet's life and his qualities of character are described by *maulvi*s. A *meelad* is in order any time that one wants to praise God and His Prophet, but it is always arranged on the birthday of the Prophet Mohammad. It is approved by orthodox Islam.

*Mehdi*   The same as the English *henna*, which was orginally a Persian word. It is a shrubbery used also as hedge around a house compound. Its leaves are mashed and applied to the palms of the hands and soles of the feet by women. The emulsion turns crimson in about two hours.

*Mehr*   A monetary consideration used in contracting marriage. The husband agrees to pay a fixed amount as *mehr* to the wife. *Mehr* is supposed to be paid before the marriage is consummated; but, in practice, the wife writes it off. However, it becomes due upon divorce.

*Mela*   Any general fair where village people gather and enjoy a day with their families buying sweets, etc. The occasion could be any annual celebration, both social and religious.

*Mir*   Chief; head.

*Mukhtiar*   A legal practitioner, but with a lower legal qualification (a certificate) than that of a lawyer.

*Munshi*   Literally, "a writer", or "a recorder." In the general sense, it has come to mean a clerical vocation, i.e., a lawyer's clerk. It is now a surname of many East Pakistani Muslim families.

*Na-banna*   A ceremony in certain parts of East Pakistan relating to the tasting of new rice.

*Na-mahram* Anyone to whom a Muslim woman could have been married but has not been married. Thus all persons with whom a marriage relationship is possible technically become *na-mahram* for a married Muslim woman, and she should not come before such persons. In actual practice in East Pakistan villages, all strangers are *na-mahram* to a Muslim woman.

*Namaz-e-Janaza* The prayers offered just before lowering the dead body into the grave. The hearse is put at a place behind which the Muslims line up and offer the prayer led by the *imam*. This prayer is also offered in the absence of the dead body if the person dies in a foreign land.

*Nawab* An official title for a big landlord.

*Nikah* The official marriage ceremony, during which a man and woman are pronounced husband and wife.

*Nishan* A sign of engagement for marriage. With a symbolic exchange of gifts, the engagement is confirmed.

*Ojha* A sorcerer who is generally called in to help persons possessed by evil spirits. He uses incantation and incense burning as part of his technique to overpower the ghost, or the witch, or the *jinn*. The services of *ojha*s are very much in demand in villages, where, because of superstitions, many diseases are attributed to possession by evil spirits.

*Pandal* A large, decorated cloth structure put up on festive occasions to accommodate guests.

*Pani-para* Water on which a religious man, after reciting certain verses, has blown his breath. The water is then believed to be blessed, and is often used by the villagers as curative for simple diseases.

*Para* A section of a village.

*Pardah* Literally, a "curtain or covering to hide something." It refers to the women's observance of being veiled against strangers.

*Patti* A section of a village divided on a geographical basis for revenue collection.

*Phirani* A return visit after the bride is brought to the house of the groom on the day of marriage.

*Peer* A religious teacher, or guide. In time this has developed into an important religious institution. Many pseudo-*peer*s came out to profit from the religious devotion of the masses, and it became difficult to discriminate between the genuine and the "quackish" *peer*s. The quacks went to the villages and enlisted the farmers as their pupils, known as *mureed*. A *peer* has numerous disciples in as many villages as his reputation can reach. In East Pakistan many such *peers* are operating even today. Genuine *peers* belong to certain religious orders, and are very strict in accepting anyone as their disciple.

*Pucca*    Any structure made of concrete and bricks, as contrasted to·mud structures.

*Puja*    Devotional prayers to various Hindu gods. The *Puja* in East Pakistan mainly relates to Durga, the goddess of sustenance, Kali, the goddess of birth and life, Laxmi, the goddess of wealth, and Sarwasati, the goddess of learning.

*Punchpitha*    Literally, "five cakes" prepared to indicate the fifth month of pregnancy. This is a local custom, and is not observed in all parts of East Pakistan.

*Pundit*    A priest called by Hindus to perform their religious ceremonies.

*Puthi*    The folk literature consisting of folk music and songs.

*Qazi*    A judge appointed to administer Muslim law. This is an old office that was sustained by the British. It now remains in use only as a family title, indicating that the original head of the family was a Muslim judge.

*Ramadan*    The month of Fasting, the ninth month of the Muslim calendar. It requires a complete abstinence from eating and drinking (including smoking and other similar habits) from dawn to dusk. Fasting is one of the five pillars of Islamic faith.

*Rupee*    Pakistan currency. It has 100 *paisas,* and is equal to U.S. 21 cents.

*Sadhu*    Hindu counterpart of *faqeer*. He is a Hindu who is supposed to have renounced the world with a view to devoting himself to the gods.

*Saiyed,* or *syed*    An Arabic word meaning "leader." Among the Muslims, those who claim their descent direct from the Prophet are known as *saiyeds*.

*Salam-O-Alaikum*    The Islamic greeting, meaning "peace be with you."

*Salis*    The arbiter in a dispute.

*Sari*    The one-piece, full-length dress for Hindu women. It is about six yards in length, and is tied around the waist.

*Sirdar*    Literally, the "leader." In East Pakistan he is an important part of the social organization. He is the presiding person on the informal village council. The *sirdar*s were a powerful force in the village sociopolitical life only a decade or so ago, and in certain parts of East Pakistan they are powerful even today. It is a hereditary institution passed on from father to oldest son.

*Sufi*  A Muslim mystic. There are a number of mystic orders, and *sufis* may be referred to the particular order. It is supposed that *sufis* have their own political organization, which is supranational, and various areas are alloted to *sufis* in order of their rank in the organization. During the Muslim rule in India, the *sufis* exerted great influence on the policies of the kings.

*Sunnah*  The sayings and the general conduct of the Prophet of Islam, also known as "the traditions." The Muslims set the *Sunnah* as the example to be followed by them.

*Taviz*  An amulet. The religious men, or saints, are requested to write the *taviz*. It is a piece of paper with certain verses of the Qur'ān inscribed on it. This paper is sewn into a tablet, and is tied on the arms or hung on the neck.

*Tola*  A measure of weight, roughly one-fortieth of a pound, used in measuring gold and silver. The next smaller unit is *masha*, there being twelve *masha* in a *tola*. There are eight *ratti* in one *masha*.

*Urs*  An annual fair at the grave of a holy man or saint. The graveyard is generally looked after by a caretaker known as the *mujawir*. People go to the *urs* and request the saint to fulfill some of their desires. When the wish is realized, they go again and make their offerings to the saint through the *mujawir*. Such offerings are used by the *mujawir*, but the poor villager is thankful all the same. Orthodox Islam does not approve of this practice.

*Zakaat*  One of the five pillars of Islamic faith, under which every solvent Muslim is required to give away annually one-fortieth of his income to charity. Under a Muslim government, this charity formed part of a charity fund with which the ruler helped the poor. *Zakaat* is a compulsory taxation, and the percentage is fixed.

*Zamindar*  A landlord. The British created this class of landlords as an intermediary between the government and the tenants. They used to be revenue collectors, and paid a certain percentage of the revenue to the government. For the tenants, they represented the rulers; and, in turn, they ruled them with a benevolent but strong hand.

*Ziarat*  A visit paid to a holy place, or holy person.

# BIBLIOGRAPHY

Arensberg, C. M., and A. H. Niehoff. *Introducing Social Change* (Chicago: Aldine Publishing Company, 1964).

Barker, R. G., T. Dembo, and K. Lewin. "Frustration and Regression: An Experiment with Children," *University of Iowa Studies in Child Welfare,* Vol. XVIII, No. 1 (1941).

Barth, F. "A Study of Pathan Organisation," *Journal of the Royal Anthropological Society,* Vol. LXXXIX (1959).

Dumont, L., and D. Pocock. *Contributions to Indian Sociology* (Paris: No. 1 [1957]).

Eglar, Z. *Punjabi Village in Pakistan* (New York: Columbia University Press, 1960).

Engel, G. L. "Homeostasis, Behavioral Adjustment and the Concept of Health and Disease," in Roy R. Grinker (ed.), *Mid-Century Psychiatry* (Illinois: 1953), pp. 33–59.

Firth, R. "Factions in Indian and Overseas Indian Societies: Introduction," *British Journal of Sociology* (1957), Vol. VIII, pp. 291–94.

Gerth, H. H., and C. W. Mills. *From Max Weber: Essays in Sociology* (London: 1947).

Honigmann, J. J. *Three Pakistan Villages* (Chapel Hill: Institute for Research in Social Sciences, University of North Carolina, 1958).

Husain, A. F. A. *Human and Social Impact of Technological Change in Pakistan,* Vol. I (Dacca: Oxford University Press, 1956).

Inayatullah. "Caste, Patti and Factions in the Life of a Punjab Village," *Sociologus,* Vol. VIII, No. 2 (1958), pp. 170–86.

Karim, A. "Impact of Islam on Bengal." Paper read in a seminar on Cultural History of East Pakistan (Dacca: *Morning News,* Magazine Section, March 14, 1965).

Karim, Nazmul. "Some Aspects of Popular Beliefs among Muslims of Bengal," *Eastern Anthropologist,* Vol. IX, No. 1 (1955), pp. 29–41.

—————. *Changing Society of India and Pakistan* (Dacca: Oxford University Press, 1961).

Katz, E., and P. F. Lazarsfeld. *Personal Influence* (New York: Free Press, 1960).

Kerr, M. *Personality and Conflict in Jamaica* (London: Collins, 1963).

Khan, A. H. *Rural Development in East Pakistan* (East Lansing: Michigan State University Asian Studies Center, 1964).

Leighton, A. H. *et al. Psychiatric Disorders among the Yoruba* (Ithaca: Cornell University Press, 1963).

Lerner, D. *The Passing of Traditional Society* (New York: Free Press, 1958).

Lewis, O. *Village Life in Northern India* (University of Illinois, 1958).

—————. *Group Dynamics in a North Indian Village* (Delhi: Planning Commission, Government of India, 1954).

Linton, R. *The Study of Man* (New York: Appleton-Century, 1936).

Maron, S. (ed). *Pakistan Society* (New Haven: Human Relations Area File, 1957).

Mayone, S. J. "Patterns of Communication in a Rural Greek Village," *Public Opinion Quarterly*, Vol. XVI (1952).

Mead, M. *Cultural Pattern and Technical Change* (New York: Anchor Books, 1955).

Morris, H. S. "Communal Rivalry among Indians in Uganda," *British Journal of Sociology*, Vol. VIII (1957), pp. 306–17.

Opler, M., and R. D. Singh. "The Division of Labor in an Indian Village," in C. C. Coon (ed.), *A Reader in General Anthropology* (New York: 1948), pp. 464–96.

Orenstein, H. *Gaon: Conflict and Cohesion in an Indian Village* (Princeton: Princeton University Press, 1965).

Pocock, D. "The Bases of Factions in Gujerat," *British Journal of Sociology*, Vol. VIII (1957), pp. 295–306.

Rahim, M. A. *Social and Cultural History of Bengal* (Karachi: Pakistan Publishing House, 1963).

Rahim, S. A. *Diffusion and Adoption of Agricultural Practices* (Comilla: East Pakistan Academy, Technical Publication No. 7 [1961]).

—————. *Communication and Personal Influence in an East Pakistan Village* (Comilla: East Pakistan Academy, 1965).

Redfield, R. *Peasant Society and Culture*. Chicago: University of Chicago Press, 1956).

Rogers, E. M. *Diffusion of Innovation* (New York: Free Press, 1962).

Sanders, I. T. "Research with Peasants in Underdeveloped Areas," *Social Forces*, Vol. XXXV (1956).

Schuler, E. A., and S. M. Hafeez Zaidi. "Response to Village Disaster: Tornado and Hailstorm at South Rampur," *Journal of the Pakistan Academy, Comilla,* Vol. II, Nos. 2 and 3 (1961), pp. 1–14, 27–41.

Siegel, B. J., and A. R. Beals, "Pervasive Factionalism," *American Anthropologist,* Vol. LXII, No. 3 (1960), pp. 394–417.

Slocum, W. L., J. Akhtar, and A. F. Sahi. *Village Life in Lahore District* (Lahore: Punjab University Social Science Research Centre, 1960).

Srinivas, M. N. "The Dominant Caste in Rampura," *American Anthropologist,* Vol. LXI, No. 1 (1959), pp. 1–16.

Spiro, M. E. "The Psychological Function of Witchcraft: The Burmese Case." Paper read at the *Conference on Mental Health in Asia and the Pacific* (Honolulu: East-West Center, 1966).

Wallace, A. F. C. *Culture and Personality* (New York: Random House, 1961).

Wiser, W. H. *The Hindu Jajmani System* (Lucknow: 1936).

Young, K. *Personality and Problems of Adjustment* (London: Kegan Paul, 1947).

Zaidi, S. M. Hafeez. "Problems of Human Relations in Industry in Pakistan," *Journal of Social Psychology,* Vol. XLIX (1959), pp. 13–18.

————. "Reactions to Stress as a Function of the Level of Intelligence," *Genetic Psychology Monographs,* Vol. LXII (1960), pp. 41–104.

————. "Pakistan: A Society in Transition," *Psychologia,* Vol. VII, No. 1 (1964), pp. 15–21.

————. "Socio-cultural Change and Value-conflict in Developing Countries: A Case-study of Pakistan." Paper read at the *Conference on Mental Health in Asia and the Pacific* (Honolulu: East-West Center, March–April, 1966).

————, and E. A. Schuler. "Reactions to Disaster in an East Pakistan Village," in J. Owen (ed.), *Sociology in East Pakistan* (Dacca: Asiatic Society of Pakistan, 1962.)